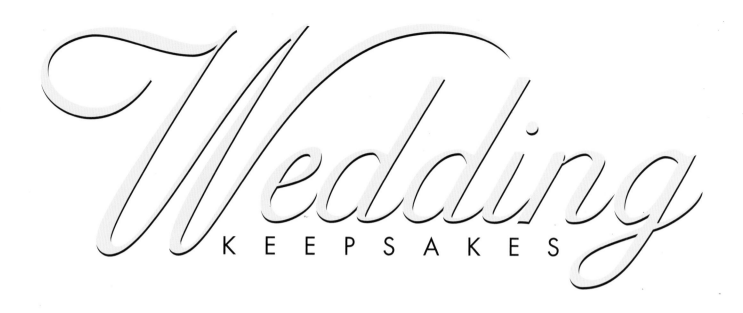

Wedding
KEEPSAKES

Siobhán McGowan

Introduction by
Lisa Bearnson

CREATING KEEPSAKES BOOKS

Orem, Utah

Published in 2000 by Creating Keepsakes Books, a division of Porch Swing Publishing, Inc., 354 South Mountain Way Drive, Orem, Utah 84058, 800/815-3538. Visit us at www.creatingkeepsakes.com

Printed in the U.S.A.

Library of Congress Cataloging-in-Publication Data

McGowan, Siobhán.
   Wedding keepsakes / Siobhán McGowan ; introduction by Lisa Bearnson.
    p. cm.
   ISBN 1-929180-17-9 — ISBN 1-929180-18-7 (pbk.)
   1. Paper work. 2. Weddings—Equipment and supplies.
3. Souvenirs (Keepsakes) 4. Scrapbooks. I. Title.
   TT870 .M39 2000
   745.594'1—dc21   00-043125

Creating Keepsakes Books may be purchased in bulk for sales promotions, premiums, or fundraisers. For information, please write to: Special Markets Department, Creating Keepsakes Books, 354 South Mountain Way Drive, Orem, Utah 84058

Creating Keepsakes Books
Editorial Office, Washington, D.C.
Director: Maureen Graney/Blackberry Press, Inc.
Art Director: Susi Oberhelman
Production Consultant: Kathy Rosenbloom
Editor: Stephanie Henke
Captions: Stephanie Henke
Editorial and Research Assistants: Annalise Rabasa, Courtney McGowan
Index: Pat Woodruff
Archival Consultant: Jeanne English
Origami diagrams, page 113: Annalise Rabasa

Principal Photography: Renée Comet Photography, Washington, D.C.
Photo, page 96: Al Thelin, Salt Lake City, Utah.
Cover: Photo by Laurence Monneret, Tony Stone Images.

Creating Keepsakes™ scrapbook magazine
Main Office, Orem, Utah
Editorial Director: Lisa Bearnson
Creative Director: Don Lambson
Publisher and CEO: Mark Seastrand

Creating Keepsakes™ scrapbook magazine is published ten times a year. To subscribe, call 888/247-5282.

Contents

Foreword

CONGRATULATIONS! You're getting married! And getting married means planning the party of a lifetime. As you prepare to take part in the civil, religious, and cultural rituals that solemnize love and commitment between two people, remember this: The best part of planning a wedding can be the chance to be creative.

Simply put, it's fun to add a personal touch to your wedding! Beautiful papers, rubber stamp designs, and scrapbooking techniques all suggest easy paper-based projects for brides, grooms, and their helpers. Among the many examples included in this book are unique invitations, creative decorations for the reception, wedding album ideas, and gifts. Be inspired to make lasting keepsakes to commemorate your special day, because family, friends, and future generations will treasure them for many years to come.

Even after your wedding is over and the last thank-you notes have been sent, we encourage you to turn to these pages for planning parties and making cards and invitations for other brides and grooms, and for crafting meaningful gifts for friends at anniversaries and other special times. But for now, we wish *you* a happy wedding day!

Introduction

WHERE WAS THIS book when I got married over a decade ago? Like all future brides, I wanted to add a personal touch to my wedding. But, preprinted invitations sporting a bright '80s photo of me and my honey was about as personal as it got! Thanks to the invaluable information on the following pages, you can now be the creative genius behind your wedding—and save thousands in the meantime.

As an avid scrapbooker, I'm excited to flip through these pages and, among the many ideas from people across the country, see invitations and wedding photos from Brenda Bennett, creative lettering and thank you notes from Heather Thatcher, and place cards and table settings by Jenny Jackson. These women are first and foremost great scrapbookers (they're all *Creating Keepsakes* "Scrapbook Hall of Famers"), but here they're using their scrapbooking skills to make beautiful and creative wedding projects.

Hats off to writer Siobhan McGowan for pulling together such a useful compilation of wedding information. From invitation and thank-you etiquette to wedding quotes, she's written a book that covers a fascinating diversity of wedding traditions as well as basics that everyone wants to know.

If you're already out of the wedding mode, this book's still for you. I plan on using several of the unique ideas for my parents fiftieth wedding anniversary celebration and the "Beach Bash" engagement party invitation for a summer "Fun in the Sun" party for the neighborhood kids!

❧ LISA BEARNSON

HEARTS CARD by Jenny Jackson. Patterned paper: Bo-Bunny Press. Punch: Marvy Uchida. Computer font: CK Script, "Best of Creative Lettering" CD Vol 1, *Creating Keepsakes*.

WEDDING CARD by Jenny Jackson. Paper: color cardstock, handmade paper by The Natural Paper Co. Stamp: Embossing Arts Co. Ribbon. Heart ornament.

FOLDER CARD by Diane Hackley. Template: Folder by American Traditional Stencils. Scissors: Fiskars. Punch. "On Your Wedding Day" stamp: Stampa Rosa. Raindrops and swirls stamp: Hero Arts. Inkpads: Encore Metallics. Ribbon: Offray.

Invitations

THE QUESTION has been asked. The answer—a joyous "yes!"—offered with a full heart. Although it may take a day or two, eventually the euphoria of that moment is tempered by thoughts of the undertaking at hand, and your mind fills with a million ideas. The reception site, the wedding dress, the seating arrangements, the catering costs—so many details demand attention. On the average bride's Top Ten list of anxiety-inducing elements, the invitation often ranks pretty close to number one, provoking flashbacks to eighth-grade grammar class and fears of etiquette faux pas. But when planning a wedding, stationery is the starting point that sets the tone for the entire event. After all, the invitation is often the first inkling a guest gets of the style of the celebration to come. And with so many wonderful options available today, from handmade petal papers to richly colored inks to evocative vellum overlays, the challenge—choosing which combination best reflects the sensibilities of you and your future husband—can be an enjoyable one.

Many paper products make up the bridal stationery, but the main components—in order of appearance—are: engagement announcement; engagement party invite; save-the-date card; wedding (and reception) invite; bridal shower and

ENGAGEMENT FIESTA FOR Lane —and— ♥AMY

Saturday, the 2nd of October at one in the afternoon. We will meet at the Elletsen's Casita. RSVP & directions to Kay & Mary 566-2299

Fiesta

♥ To Celebrate Ron & Lisa's Engagement
♥ When? Saturday, October 2nd at 2 P.M.
♥ Where? Catalina Park · RSVP 566-2299

Engagement Picnic For Beth & Scott Sat. June 1ST·1pm Sandia Park

BEACH BASH INVITATIONS by Lanae Johnson. Patterned paper: Kangaroo and Joey. Palm tree die cut: Mara-mi. Adhesive: Sailor Glue Pen; Photo Mounts, Creative Memories. Inflatable beach ball: Oriental Trading Co. Fun idea to note: Lanae carefully arranged her lettered blocks and the die-cut palm tree to create this festive invitation. For multiple copies, color copy your original or scan it in to a computer and make multiple printouts on a color printer. Lanae brought the fun to the envelope, too, by adhering a beach-ball die-cut to the envelope flap. For extra impact, you could add an inflatable beach ball. Insert it into an oversize envelope with the invitation attached, or inflate the ball for those hand-delivered invitations!

ENGAGEMENT FIESTA by Lanae Johnson. Patterned paper: Cactus & Peppers, Sonburn. Pens: Micron Pigma, Sakura; Artist Pigmented Pen, Marvy Uchida. Adhesive: Sailor Glue Pen; Photo Mounts, Creative Memories. Fun idea to note: Lanae coordinated her colors with the patterned paper and did her lettering on the same background color. She created a fun and colorful collage by using borders of various colors and widths and by angling and overlapping her lettering blocks.

FIESTA by Lanae Johnson. Paper: MM's Design. Pen: Micron Pigma, Sakura. Scissors: Deckle edge trimmer, Family Treasures.

WATERMELON SLICE by Lanae Johnson. Paper: Frances Meyer. Pen: Micron Pigma, Sakura. Colored pencil: Prisma. Fun idea to note: Lanae created a master copy of the lettering by forming the letters on a piece of paper; she then placed it on a light box to use as a guide as she hand-lettered each invitation.

bachelor party invites; wedding announcement; and thank-you notes. Central among these is the wedding invitation. Although delicately worded and dressed up in distinctive wrappings, the information conveyed by the invitation serves a simple, straightforward function. It tells the recipient who is hosting the wedding, and when and where the wedding

will take place. Depending upon how elaborate the ensuing celebration will be, a well-designed and all-inclusive invitation has an RSVP card with a corresponding stamped, self-addressed envelope and a variety of enclosures concerning, for example, assigned seating at the church or synagogue, alternate venues in case of inclement weather, and maps indicating the way from the ceremony to the reception site. Of course, the invitation is also a very special request for the guest to share in the occasion.

The purpose of the other stationery elements may seem self-evident, but various vagaries of decorum do apply. After you've shared the news first with your parents and then, by phone or by personal letter, with your closest friends and family members, an engagement announcement officially notifies your wider circle of relatives and acquaintances—cousins, coworkers, and the like. The printed announcement can be as formal or informal as you wish. It need not match the style of your invitation stationery, since chances are you've yet to determine just what that is. And even if you do already know the wedding date, don't include it, or any other specifics of the upcoming ceremony. The engagement announcement is merely a declaration of your intention to marry. Note: It is not a call for gifts! In fact, the only correspondence that can refer to the couple's registry is the bridal shower invitation.

An engagement party launches the year (or six months, or two years) of activities leading up to the actual wedding day. Whether in addition to or in lieu of an engagement announcement, an engagement party is a sociable way to spread the word and celebrate. Engagement parties can center on a variety of themes, from a casual backyard barbecue to a dressy evening reception, and the formality of the invitation should reflect the formality of the gathering. But when it comes to wording, etiquette dictates that guests are invited to a party "in honor of" Jack and Jill.

If a significant number of guests will need to make special travel arrangements in order to attend the nuptials, if the wedding will take place in a popular part of the country during peak tourist season, or if the wedding will be held on a holiday, it's courteous to send a save-the-date card many months in advance. Cards can be short, but to spare any confusion, they should include a sentence to the effect of "Invitation to Follow."

According to tradition, the maid of honor hosts the bridal shower, although modern brides often benefit from several different showers—separate parties held by friends, coworkers, classmates, and so on. Bridal showers can be held on any day of the week, at any time of the day—a Friday lunch at the office, an afternoon at a girlfriend's apartment— but it's best to make the date within two weeks to two months of the wedding. Any sooner, and the shower runs the risk of preceding a cancellation of the nuptials due to a change in plans; any later, and it may interfere with last-minute preparations. One final scheduling caveat: Shower invites ideally should be sent after those for the ceremony—that way, the tone for the wedding will have been set by the invitation, and the shower stationery can be more casual.

The bridal shower invitation differs from other invitations because guests count on it to indicate what gifts to buy. That's why it's perfectly okay for shower stationery to cite the couple's color preferences, the store at which they're registered, and, if relevant to the theme, the bride's clothing sizes. In fact, the bridal shower (and bachelor party) invitations offer the biggest opportunity to get wild, crazy, and creative. Pick a theme, then take it to the extreme: A pajama party invite could accompany a

beauty kit containing a mud mask, fuzzy bunny slippers, and cheeky retro hair rollers. Coy messages printed on scented paper fans trailing suggestive satin ribbons might provide just the touch of modesty required at a sexy lingerie shower. A hardbound edition of a romantic tome—be it a volume of verse by Edna St. Vincent Millay, a juvenile favorite by Judy Blume, or just about anything by Jane Austen—

BACKYARD B-B-Q by Lanae Johnson. Paper: Mara-mi. Lettering template: Funky, Journaling Genie #3. Pen: Micron Pigma, Sakura. Fun idea to note: You can reduce or enlarge Journaling Genie shapes to suit your particular design. Lanae recommends that you first practice your lettering on tracing paper before creating an original that can be reproduced on a computer or copier.

WEDDING ROUND-UP by Lanae Johnson. Paper: Creative Papers, C.R. Gibson. Pen: Micron Pigma, Sakura. Fun idea to note: Choose words for the invitation that reflect your party's theme; here, Lanae used "round-up," "Bar-B-Q," and "high noon" to reflect her western theme. To create multiple copies of the invitation, use a black-and-white copier to copy your original letters onto cardstock, or create your lettering on the computer and then print them directly onto cardstock.

AMIGOS WANTED by Lanae Johnson. Template: Oval. Pen: Micron Pigma, Sakura. Scissors: Deckle edge trimmer. Lettering: "Wanted" adapted from Penny Laine Papers. Fun idea to note: Lanae created various lettering blocks to make this tri-fold invitation very festive! She mounted her letters on colored cardstock to create borders and then adhered them to a tri-fold card. Because her colors are simple, the invitation isn't too busy.

with details of the shower tucked between the pages on a commemorative bookmark would provide guests with something to talk about. The ideas, and creative ways to announce them, are endless.

Women-only showers are still the status quo, but an ever-increasing number of non-traditionalists now advocate coed showers that also involve the groom. This is particularly true if the couple hosting the party is friendly with both the bride and her beau. For such reasons, it's not only unnecessary but often downright difficult to throw a surprise shower. Except in the case of an extremely small circle of family and friends, the host almost always has to consult with the bride in order to determine the guest list. In the case of multiple showers, the bride needs to cross-reference that same list in order to ensure her friends are not overburdened by several separate requests for presents.

Hosted by the best man for the husband-to-be, a bachelor party is the men's equivalent of a bridal shower. Invitations follow the same time schedule—and it goes without saying that a bachelor party the night before the wedding is a bad idea (any marriage that starts off with the groom asleep at the altar . . .). If your guy is feeling creative, suggest that he and his buddies become documentary film directors for a rowdy weekend by videotaping their road-trip antics, a local rock concert, or an open-mic night at a comedy club. The invite, illustrated like an oversized movie ticket, could accompany a canister of film, a black beret, and a bag of microwave popcorn. Whether the party entails a wilderness trek, a softball tournament, or a visit to a virtual-reality arcade, the invite can be custom-designed to promote the theme.

Wedding announcements are sent after the ceremony to anyone who is not invited to the nuptials but whom the couple would like to inform of

AROUND THE CLOCK by Lanae Johnson. Clock die cut: Mara Mi. Pen: Micron Pigma, Sakura. Adhesive: Sailor Glue Pen; Photo Mounts, Creative Memories. Fun idea to note: By angling the block of lettering against the striped background, Lanae created an energetic invitation!

CLOCKS AND WATCHES by Lanae Johnson. Patterned paper: Coloriginals. Pen: Micron Pigma, Sakura. Fun idea to note: Lanae incorporated the clock theme in her lettering of the "o"s in the words "Around" and "Clock" as an extra-special touch.

CARD SHOWER FOR AMBER NICOLE by Lanae Johnson. Pen: Micron Pigma, Sakura. Fun idea to note: This announcement of a card shower is also a great way to share the exciting news of an engagement.

DEVIN'S LUAU by Lanae Johnson. Patterned paper: Amscan. Punch: small hole. Pens: Artist, Marvy Uchida; Micron Pigma, Sakura. Colored pencils: Prisma. Adhesive: Sailor Glue Pen; Photo Mounts, Creative Memories. Leis or party favor umbrellas. Fun idea to note: Lanae created this original design by using lots of fun colors and lettering. Letters could be created by hand and filled in with colored pencil, or created using computer fonts. Lanae mounted blocks of text onto contrasting cardstock and trimmed them unevenly with scissors. Next, she overlapped these shapes and mounted them to the patterned paper. Then she mounted this to purple stock, creating a border. Lanae made copies on a color copier, but the original could also have been scanned into a computer and printed out on a color printer. One version of this invitation had two holes punched so a party-favor umbrella could be inserted. Another variation was mailed in a box with a lei!

their marriage. Print, address, and stamp announcements in advance of the wedding, but don't post them until the day after the ceremony. Ask a bridesmaid or close family member to do the honor of dropping them in the mailbox.

Formal, Semiformal, Informal

The date is set and the location chosen. Now how to put it on paper? When it comes to style, the invitation should encapsulate, in parcel-post format, the atmosphere you intend to create on the day itself. Think of the invitation as a way of giving your guests a clue to all the special things to come—the epistolary equivalent of dropping a hint.

Both the design and the wording of an invitation determine whether it is formal, semiformal, or informal. The formal invitation is socially correct in

every way: It is written in the third person ("Mr. and Mrs. Jonathan Thomas Rockefeller request the honour of your presence . . .") and printed (technically, engraved) in black or dark gray ink on white or ecru stock, which may be flat, in the form of a stiff, round-cornered card, or vertically folded. If flat, the card may be beveled with gold or silver. If folded, the trim when closed can be one of two standard sizes: classic (4½ x 6 inches), or embassy (5⅛ x 7¼ inches). Very formal invites even allow a space for the name of the recipient to be written in by hand. A formal invitation, topped by a protective square of tissue paper, is mailed, along with the response card and any other enclosures, inside two envelopes, the inner of which has no glue, and is not sealed.

A semiformal invitation may still adhere to convention in its phrasing and overall packaging, but the particulars of its design are more artful. For example, a semiformal invitation may feature ink in shades of rich burgundy, royal blue, or deep teal. The typeface may be more modern. Handmade petal papers may unfold to reveal a printed card. Although the trim may be traditional, the edges may be ragged. It's the playful balance between formality

ROSE BRIDAL SHOWER INVITATION by Lanae Johnson. Card and envelope: Splendor Square, Paper Direct. Pens: Artist Pigmented pen, Marvy Uchida; Micron Pigma, Sakura. Fun idea to note: The card and envelope set comes with an organza white ribbon, but Lanae used a gold-and-white ribbon to create a more formal look. You could also use this design for wedding invitations or thank yous.

GOLD SWIRL BRIDAL SHOWER INVITATION by Lanae Johnson. Paper: Canford Gold. Vellum: Current. Envelopes: Glitz Cachet, Paper Direct. Adhesive: Mounting Adhesive sheets, Keep A Memory, Therm O Web. Fun idea to note: Lanae chose a casual, swirly lettering style that repeats the swirls on the invitation's envelope. She printed her message on vellum, and created the corner slits by hand, though an extended-reach punch would be more efficient for lots of invitations. For an extra touch, address your envelopes with a metallic gold pen.

BRIDAL TEA FOR JESSICA by Lanae Johnson. Paper: MM's Designs. Pen: Micron Pigma, Sakura. Colored pencils: Prisma. Fun idea to note: Lanae drew the letters by hand, placed them on a lightbox, and then traced them onto the invitation's patterned paper.

BRIDAL TEA FOR JAENA KAE by Lanae Johnson. Tea cup die cut: Mara-Mi. Pens: Micron Pigma, Sakura; Artist pigmented pen, Marvy Uchida. Adhesive: Sailor Glue Pen; Photo Mounts, Creative Memories. Fun idea to note: In her lettering, Lanae repeated the flower design from the teacup. She mounted her lettering blocks onto torn-edge purple stock, and then mounted this at angles onto lavender stock. To finish the invitation, she overlapped and adhered the teacup. Lanae repeated the teacup on the envelope flap as a pleasing teaser.

Join us for a
Bridal Shower
in honor of
Amber Nicole
We will meet
At Mimi's Cafe
June 26 · noon

A BRIDAL
TEA
for
JESSICA

Please join us
Sat, June the first
at 1:30 P.M.
at the
Savoy Tea House
to honor
the bride-to-be

Regrets only

A Bridal
TEA
for
Jaena Kae

❀ The Spicery Tea House

❀ June 7th, 2000
2:30 P.M.

❀ R.S.V.P.
to Lisa

and informality that marks a semiformal invitation.

Informal, or individualistic, invitations throw caution to the wind and embrace creativity in everything from materials to graphic motifs. They may be custom-made to complement the couple and their wedding day. An informal invitation might incorporate a lace overlay cut from the mother-of-the-bride's veil, a photograph of the couple, or a watercolor illustration of an image that holds symbolic meaning to the two—anything from a ruby-throated hummingbird to a baseball mitt. To underscore the unconventional nature of the invite, it may be printed on transparent acrylic, tinted vellum, milky glassine, or corrugated kraft paper. It may be single-, double-, or triple-folded, refer to the bride and groom by their childhood nicknames, include the lyrics to their favorite tune—"'S

Wonderful," "Autumn in New York," or "I Am The Walrus." Informal invitations may be strikingly original but don't let the label fool you: Informal does not necessarily equal casual or, heaven forbid, careless. Elegant accents and a harmonious color palette give the invite a polished appearance, and the phrasing—even if it is more relaxed than Emily Post might approve of—should be proofed twice or thrice for grammar and spelling mistakes.

Creating a Color Scheme

Choosing a color palette is one of the most intimidating prospects of designing your own wedding. When faced with the challenge of selecting a few key shades that will forever represent one of the most important days in her life, even an artistic bride can get cold feet. Maybe she loves purple, but fears it's too wild for a church wedding. Maybe she favors the warm, burnished hues of autumn, but she's getting married in May. Maybe she should just play it safe, and stick to an all-white scenario.

Because color is a subtle, yet strong, way to connect one element to another—the invitation to the wedding ceremony's program to the reception's place cards, for example—the palette plays a central role in unifying the entire event. Plus, color packs an emotional punch: Whether it's the innocence of pale pink, the tranquillity of periwinkle blue, or the energy of zesty orange, each shade evokes an immediate, instinctive response.

To determine your color scheme, don't overlook the obvious. Silly as it might sound, sit down with your fiancé and list your favorites. Which shades makes you happy? Which ones remind you of your love? If you met on a blind date for Valentine's

YOU'RE INVITED by Jenny Jackson. Paper: Hero Arts. Computer fonts: CK Contemporary Capitals and CK Journaling, "Best of Creative Lettering" CD Vol 1, *Creating Keepsakes*. Ribbon.

ANTIQUE SHOE by Kelly Edgerton. Paper: Hero Arts Note Card. Antique shoe: Wallies Prepasted Wallpaper. Stickers: Scalloped Lace Border, Mrs. Grossman's Paper Whispers. Scissors: Small Victorian, Fiskars. Computer font: CK Swirl, "Wedding Alphabet" CD, *Creating Keepsakes*.

ROSE BRIDAL SHOWER INVITATION by Kelly Edgerton. Paper: Hero Arts Note Card. Stickers: Red Rosy Border Set, PrintWorks Studio Collection. Computer font: CK Roses, "Wedding Alphabet" CD, *Creating Keepsakes*. Fun idea to note: Kelly used red for fill pattern 1 of her letters and green for fill pattern 2.

PINK TAG INVITATION by Diane Hackley. Patterned paper: Lasting Impressions. Tag: Hero Arts. Stamp: Personal Stamp Exchange. Ribbon: Offray.

PINK STRIPED INVITATION by Lanae Johnson. Patterned paper: Mara-mi (pink stripes); Frances Meyer (floral). Punch: small hole. Pencil: Prismacolor, Berol. Other: tulle, floral pins. Fun idea to note: This is a very quick and easy invitation to make! You can create a master of your lettering by hand or on the computer, and then make as many duplicates as you need by copying onto striped paper. Lanae folded the floral piece of paper in half, positioned it at the top of the card, and punched two holes. She threaded tulle through the holes and added a decorative floral pin for the finishing touch.

REHEARSAL PICNIC by Lanae Johnson. Patterned paper: Frances Meyer. Pig die cut: Mara-mi. Pen: Artist, Marvy. Adhesive: Photo Mounts, Creative Memories. Fun idea to note: Lanae filled in her block letter forms with an easy-to-draw checkered pattern that mimics the pattern of the paper (to create the checks pattern, just make rows of horizontal and vertical lines). Lanae used a black envelope and a die-cut pig on the envelope flap to draw the guest's attention to this unusual piece of mail.

FIESTA REHEARSAL DINNER by Lanae Johnson. Patterned paper: Mara-mi. Chili pepper die cut: Mara-mi. Pen: Micron Pigma, Sakura. Adhesive: Photo Mounts, Creative Memories. Fun idea to note: Lanae positioned the invitation's message at an angle, with the chili pepper overlapping, to create a dynamic design. As a postal appetizer, Lanae repeated the invitation's chili pepper die cut on the envelope flap.

Day, passionate red may be the perfect accent for an otherwise winter-white palette. Also take into account those shades that celebrate your heritage.

It's always smart to work with Mother Nature. If your palette complements the season, she'll provide you with free reinforcements—color-coordinated flowers, fruits, and foliage. Because you'll be designing your stationery many months in advance of your wedding day, this may seem like a remote concept, but keep the big picture in mind. Generally, pastels symbolize the soft, blossoming springtime. Bright primary colors can hold their own under the summer sun. Rich earthen shades and glittering jewel tones enhance autumn's blazing glory, while pure white, deep evergreen, and ornate silver and gold embellish winter's stark landscape.

After you've established your preferred hues, consult a color wheel (available at any crafts store) and consider following one of these four techniques:

☞ **White + One:** Classic white accented with just one color, in varying degrees of intensity, makes for a clean, modern look.

- Gradational Color: This technique also revolves around use of a single color, but instead of accenting a neutral, it stands on its own. From the palest to the deepest tone, use the entire A-to-Z of the shade.

- Neighboring Shades: Next-door neighbors on the color wheel—blues and lavenders, for example, or greens and yellows—are members of the same family and can be combined without clashing. Just don't choose colors at their most intense: Vary their range.

- Opposites: The contrast of opposites can make a powerful statement, but primary colors, like royal blue and ice-hockey orange, bring to mind state flags and, yes, sports team logos. Instead, take softer, more subtle variations of the same shades, and further mute them with an equalizing neutral.

If your heart is set on a traditionally styled invitation—white stock, black ink—but you still want to inject a splash of color into the formality, toss in a colored tissue insert.

BILLIARD BACHELOR PARTY by Lanae Johnson. Paper: Coloriginals. Pens: Artist pigmented pen, Marvy Uchida; Micron Pigma, Sakura. Adhesive: Photo Mounts, Creative Memories. Fun idea to note: Lanae varied the sizes and styles of her lettering to create a festive bachelor party invitation.

GAME ROOM BACHELOR PARTY by Lanae Johnson. Fun idea to note: To make multiple copies of this hand-lettered invitation, use a black-and-white copy machine to create copies directly onto the pre-designed cards.

JAKE'S VEGAS BACHELOR PARTY by Lanae Johnson. Paper: Coloriginals. Pen: Micron Pigma, Sakura. Fun idea to note: Lanae draws attention to several important words in the invitation by making them bigger than other words and putting them in capitals.

CONFETTI BACHELOR PARTY by Kelly Edgerton. Paper: Hero Arts Note Card. Stickers: Mrs. Grossman's. Pens: Gelly Roll, Sakura. Computer font: CK Contemporary, "Wedding Alphabet" CD, *Creating Keepsakes*.

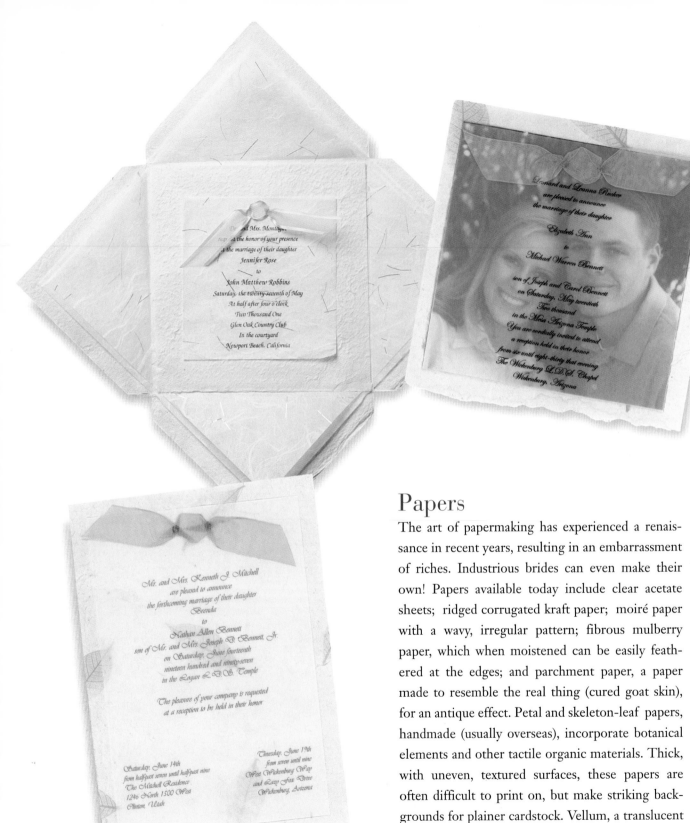

Papers

The art of papermaking has experienced a renaissance in recent years, resulting in an embarrassment of riches. Industrious brides can even make their own! Papers available today include clear acetate sheets; ridged corrugated kraft paper; moiré paper with a wavy, irregular pattern; fibrous mulberry paper, which when moistened can be easily feathered at the edges; and parchment paper, a paper made to resemble the real thing (cured goat skin), for an antique effect. Petal and skeleton-leaf papers, handmade (usually overseas), incorporate botanical elements and other tactile organic materials. Thick, with uneven, textured surfaces, these papers are often difficult to print on, but make striking backgrounds for plainer cardstock. Vellum, a translucent cotton-wood pulp blend with a matte finish, is used as either an overlay or as the actual invitation.

In addition to cost, there are two key factors to consider when choosing paper: The first, of course, is style—picking the paper that best reflects the ambiance of your planned wedding; the second is preservability. Depending on the makeup of the paper, it will yellow, age, and biodegrade over time.

"Many brides want to keep a copy of their invitation for posterity," explains Jeanne English, preservation consultant to *Creating Keepsakes* magazine. "To ensure that paper does not yellow, it's essential to use acid-free, lignin-free stationery. Lignin is the substance that gives plants their strength. It binds fibers. Whenever paper contains raw product—petals, for example—it contains lignin." Handmade papers, which are some of the prettiest available, unfortunately fall into this category. "Some handmade papers include everything from dried grass to discarded cigarette wrappers. These are never acid free." Vellum, too, fails the acid test.

Brides should also be aware that papers promoted as "pure rag" are not necessarily acid free. "Manufacturers are required to put a certain percentage of cotton in the paper in order for it to qualify as 'rag,' but once they meet that requirement, they can also add wood pulp, which will deteriorate." And the water used in the papermaking process affects the purity of the paper: Water containing everyday contaminants will contribute to the paper's eventual aging. So what's a girl to do?

BRENDA AND NATHAN'S INVITATION by Brenda Bennett. Invitation: from a kit by The Natural Paper Co. with natural mulberry floral paper and translucent European vellum.

JENNIFER AND JOHN'S INVITATION provided by The Natural Paper Co. Paper: Natural mulberry skeleton leaf paper, The Natural Paper Co. Punch: small hole. Computer font: Vivaldi, MS Word. Ribbon: Stampin' Up!

ELIZABETH AND MICHAEL, PICTURED TOGETHER by Brenda Bennett. Paper: Natural mulberry skeleton leaf paper, The Natural Paper Co. Punch: small hole. Computer font: Edwardian Script ITC, MS Word. Ribbon: Stampin' Up! Fun idea to note: Brenda created the invitation's message on the computer and printed it directly onto vellum. After the ink dried, she placed the vellum over a computer printout of a sepia-toned photograph. She centered these over the mulberry paper, punched holes through all layers, and tied the three sheets together with ribbon.

JENNIFER AND RICHARD'S INVITATION provided by The Natural Paper Co. Paper: Natural mulberry floral paper, The Natural Paper Co. Vellum: Translucent European, The Natural Paper Co. Ribbon.

Mr. and Mrs. Geoffrey Williamson
request the pleasure of your company
at the marriage of their daughter
Jennifer Anne
to
Mr. Richard Bryant
Saturday, the twenty-ninth of May
Nineteen hundred and ninety-nine
at two o'clock in the afternoon
The Courtyard
Fashion Island
Newport Beach, California

Reception following the ceremony

"Printers—not neighborhood copy shops, but true stationers—have sample books that specify the acid and lignin levels in each type of paper, and can recommend high quality papers," English advises. "Also, sprays such as Archival Mist help to preserve printed materials by neutralizing their acid content."

Then again, a bride may decide that momentary beauty is more important than museum quality. "In my experience, I find that most brides are primarily concerned with design issues," admits Lisa Ben-Dror, head of the Paper by the Pound division of Kate's Paperie in New York City. "Vellum is very popular for invitations. Women like to layer tinted vellum on top of handmade paper, so that the pattern of the handmade paper—petals, fronds, hemp, mulberry, and other organic materials—is veiled. Textured papers really appeal to the senses. We've even offered one that had seeds mixed into the pulp: If you planted it in the garden and poured water over it, it literally would grow!"

Motifs and Embellishments

Seeds, petals, watercolor paintings, photographs, monograms, ribbon trims: With so many accessories available, it's tempting to dress up stationery with all sorts of trinkets. But although a bachelor party or shower announcement can pull off an ornamental look, when it comes to the actual wedding invitation, style-sensitive brides would be wise to swear by the dictum *less is more*. Consider that the invitation is a relatively small piece of paper to begin with, that it serves an informative purpose and will be dominated by type, and that, depending on your decisions, you're already making an impact with your color palette and your choice of papers. The best reason to embellish your invitation is to further emphasize the bond between you and your beloved. Otherwise, such accents may seem gratuitous.

One of the most interesting ways to subtly personalize an invitation is to feature a motif, and carry that motif through all aspects of the ceremony and reception. Your motif can be any small icon that holds special meaning to you and your fiancé. Classic wedding symbols include a tiny tiered cake or two interlocked rings. Happy harbingers of the season—a sunflower for summer, a maple leaf for fall, a cluster of holly berries for winter—can also be quite charming, as can simple depictions of the wedding site—a quaint chapel, a historic lighthouse, a rustic footbridge. Less literal images might convey a message: an acorn could represent the seedling of a marriage meant to grow strong; a sailboat, the journey ahead. Bumblebees, butterflies, the owl and the pussycat, the dish and the spoon: Motifs can evoke a treasured childhood tale, a shared passion, or any emotional touchstone that will remind you—and your guests—just why you're meant to be together. In general, a small, simplified symbol has the most impact. Too much detail will distract from the invitation as a whole.

A monogram is a traditional wedding motif, but some caveats apply to its usage. Even if the bride plans to take her husband's name, or both the bride and groom's last names coincidentally begin with the same initial, it's still considered inappropriate to use a three-letter monogram on the invitation, because the couple is not yet married. It's also poor manners to employ a monogram if the wedding will be hosted by the bride's parents or both sets of parents—basically anyone other than the bride and groom. After all, the invitation is being issued by the hosts, and the stationery should not detract from this fact. But if you and your fiancé are hosting your own wedding, you could choose to feature a less traditional monogram comprised of either four initials—your and his first and last—or, if the ceremony and reception are to be informal, two first initials: "M & D."

After you've determined the motif, the next step is to decide how to reproduce it. Your options

MEGAN AND RUSSELL'S INVITATION by Kristy Banks. Templates: Pebbles in My Pocket. Font: CK Calligraphy, "Best of Creative Lettering" CD Vol 1, *Creating Keepsakes.* Ribbon.

LACEY AND ANTHONY'S INVITATION by Lacey Sievers. Paper: Paper Complements/Crafter's Workshop (sage); Provo Craft (floral). Vellum: Accent Design. Stickers: Me & My Big Ideas. Computer fonts: DJ Sketched and DJ Calligraphy, DJ Inkers.

KIMBERLY AND JAY'S INVITATION by Theresa Cifali/Crafter's Workshop. Petal paper: handmade by Sharon Kaplan. Punch: 1/16" hole, McGill. Computer font: Dahrlin. Raffia ribbon. Fun idea to note: Theresa often uses computer fonts created by Canon and Microsoft.

NANCY AND RICHARD'S INVITATION by Theresa Cifali/Crafter's Workshop. Paper: Paper Complements/Crafter's Workshop (sponged); Frances Meyer (floral). Premium cover paper: Marco's. Metallic paper: The Paper Cut. Computer font: Tolkien. Adhesive: ATG 700 Glue Tape.

The honour of your presence is requested
at the marriage of
Miss Nancy Sue Mitchell
and
Richard Paul Miller
on Saturday, the ninth of August
two thousand
at three o'clock in the afternoon

Church of Christ
1500 Bayberry Street
Niles, Ohio

With the moons and stars as their witnesses please join Joanna Lynn Armstrong and Daniel Martin Lewis along with their parents as they unite under the heavens on Saturday, the thirteenth of March two thousand at seven o'clock in the evening

James House Tarrytwon, New York

Mr. and Mrs. Douglas B. Wadsworth Are pleased to announce The marriage of their daughter Jennifer To Brock C. Jackson Son of Mr. and Mrs. Eric C. Jackson On Friday, the twentieth of December, Nineteen hundred and ninety-one The pleasure of your company is requested at a reception held in their honor six until nine o'clock Heritage House South 2000 East

You are cordially invited to attend the wedding ceremony at Nine o'clock in the Salt Lake Temple. Please arrive 20 minutes early.

are numerous; let the tone of your wedding be the guide. In blind embossing, paper is imprinted so that a raised relief of the motif decorates the surface. The motif is not colored; its artfulness lies in the impression. Gold embossing is like blind embossing, but the impression is layered with thin gold leaf or other metallic foil. With a die-cut, the pattern of the motif is cut out of the paper, turning it into a miniature stencil through which the background appears. Custom-made die-cuts can be expensive, but ready-made dies and punches are available at craft stores, and a stencil, along with a utility knife and a steady hand, can be used for simple, framing shapes. Inks or watercolors illustrate the motif in pretty, impressionistic brush strokes. If your list is only 25 names long, the special effort required to hand-paint each invitation will reward each of your loved ones with a small work of art—but if you plan to celebrate with 500 of your closest friends, you'll have to get started years in advance! On stamps, a relief of the motif is carved out of rubber, then coated in ink and pressed on the paper. It's relatively inexpensive to order a custom-made rubber stamp, but remember that this style of decoration is best suited to semiformal and informal invitations. The inked, unfinished stamp edges left behind on thick, fiber-flecked paper might perfectly capture the rustic, rough-hewn feel of an outdoor country wedding, but would look sloppy on a streamlined, minimalist, urban-chic invite. Books, discs, or CDs of computer clip art offer hundreds of motif options that can be scanned or down-loaded, placed in a computer document, then printed on stationery.

Motifs are not the only way to customize stationery. Embossing or stamps can also create borders. Ribbons can be added as accents or used to tie together the invitation and all the enclosures. Photographs of the happy couple, the bride and

groom as children, the wedding site, or a beautiful image such as a rose blossom, make eye-catching backgrounds for a printed vellum overlay. For a romantic, hand-torn effect, deckle paper edges with the aid of special scissors or rotary cutters (available at craft stores). Deckling works best on medium-to-thick handmade papers; vellum can be scissor-cut, but because it is so thin it cracks easily.

Computer Typefaces and Point Size

From the classic line of Albertan Inline to the declarative Flemish Script or the sweet Chanson d'Amour, every typeface makes its own impact:

Nuptial Script

ALBERTAN INLINE

Flemish Script

Mona Lisa Recut

Chanson d'Amour

MOON AND STARS INVITATION by Theresa Cifali/Crafter's Workshop. Patterned paper: Colors by Design. Scissors: Colonial Charm by Family Treasures. Computer font: Draconian. Adhesive: ATG 700 Glue Tape.

HEARTS by Jenny Jackson. Template: Lasting Impressions for Paper. Computer font: CK Script, "Best of Creative Lettering" CD Vol. 1, *Creating Keepsakes*.

WINTER SNOWFLAKES by Cathy Arnold. Paper: Halcraft USA. Punch: small hole. Computer font: CAC Leslie. Other: plastic snowflake, white polyester craft ribbon, plastic/mylar snowflake confetti. Fun idea to note: Cathy lettered her invitations on the computer. Once they were printed, she punched a hole at the top, threaded a ribbon through, and tied a snowflake to the invitation. As an added festive touch, Cathy placed snowflake confetti inside the invitation's envelope!

Most word processing programs come with a limited set of alphabets, but more can easily be purchased on CD from computer software outlets. Register with manufacturers to receive mailings that will notify you of upgrades to programs such as Microsoft Word, Pagemaker, or Quark. Art supply stores and design-school book shops are also excellent places to browse. Both will offer brochures and booklets about innovations in typography, and these will include mail-in cards, 800 numbers, or Internet addresses to contact for more information. In fact, most fonts can be ordered over the Internet and delivered as an e-mail attachment. Search under the key word "font" to find all sorts of websites that allow you to download for free. Each manufacturer labels its fonts with different names, so to find your ideal, it's just a question of trial and error.

In addition to experimenting with type style, you'll also want to review type, or "point," size. Most everyday text is set in 10-point or 12-point type, but these sizes are not always the best choices; this varies according to the alphabet. A 12-point Times Roman font, for example, will be smaller than a 12-point Palatino font. Too-small type is uncomfortable to read; too-large type is ungainly. Determine point size based on the amount of information you want to include within the parameters of your paper. For a clean design, frame text blocks with spacious margins and allow plenty of breathing room between lines.

Printing at Home

Inkjet and laser printers are perfectly capable of creating crisp documents. Depending on the length of your guest list, print the entire invitation quantity on your chosen paper or a master on a bright white sheet (it makes the type look its sharpest). The master can then be photocopied onto stationery.

Before printing in bulk, run a sample, read it yourself, and have two other eagle-eyed friends check it as well. (Any editor knows that the most obvious mistakes are the easiest to miss.) When you are ready to print, pace your home printer: Printing en masse takes its toll on a machine. The ink may smudge, leave behind lines, or fail to fill in all the letters. Check each page for imperfections and decide which ones you can live with, which ones demand a do-over. When photocopying, print extras as a precautionary measure.

Just as you can choose your font, you can customize the ink color to set the mood of a page. Review your printer manual for instructions on how to order colored ink and change cartridges. As with paper, there are archival issues to consider when it comes to ink. Jeanne English explains, "Laser printers usually use powder toners, which create permanent ink,

LOVE by Lanae Johnson. Adhesive: Photo Mounts, Creative Memories. Fun idea to note: Lanae created the lettering on her computer and printed the invitations directly onto gold cardstock. By mounting this onto black cardstock, she created a defining, narrow black border. Lanae cut a square window into the envelope, which peeks at the invitation's design. She also cut the envelope flap to a shorter length, so that it ends where the die cut window begins. Lanae coordinated her reply card with the invitation by using the same decorative letter design.

AMY AND LANE by Lanae Johnson. Adhesive: glue pen. Fun idea to note: Lanae created her lettering on the computer, and printed it directly onto white cardstock. She mounted this onto black, then gold, to create an elegant border. She repeated this same design for the reply cards.

whereas inkjet printers often use liquid cartridges, which produce water-soluble type. In time, inkjet printing will fade, and if exposed to moisture, will bleed." To determine the status of your printer, run a sample printout under water to see if type smudges.

Specialty papers may also pose problems to home printers. Due to their thickness (petal paper) or surface (vellum), they may not make it through the machine intact, and embedded or metallicized papers can leave behind tiny fragments which will damage equipment. To have your cake and eat it, too, print text on plain, high-quality cardstock and then mount it onto more ornate papers.

Wording Etiquette

Like taxes, the issue of invitation etiquette can only be ignored for so long. For a few seemingly innocent and well-intentioned phrases, enough rules apply to fill entire books. If you're a real stickler, or if your family dynamics are real sticky, consult a couple of them. Having said that . . .

Formally worded invites abbreviate or punctuate almost nothing. Titles such as "Mrs." and "Jr." are exceptions. Street and state names are spelled out. So are numerals in addresses, dates, and times. "Half after" or "half past" are used in lieu of "-thirty," and it's acceptable to add "in the afternoon" or "in the evening," but "a.m." and "p.m." are verboten. Commas only appear between days and dates ("Wednesday, the twenty-first of June") and between cities and states ("Lakeview, Florida"). With the exception of proper nouns, no words are capitalized.

Although the year is considered mandatory on announcements, invitations do not require it.

However, especially now that we've crossed the threshold into Y2K, many brides will want to include it. The most formal wording would be "two thousand and two." "Twenty hundred and three" may sound a bit thick on the tongue, but it's in keeping with last century's familiar format, "nineteen hundred and ninety-nine."

The first line of a formal invitation states the names of the hosts—whatever combination of parents, step-parents, or no parents that may mean. Divorced folks are placed on separate lines. Numerous dictates govern the use of the mother's first name, depending on whether she is married, separated, divorced, professionally titled, or hosting the wedding. For very delicate situations, general language—"Together with their families"—avoids the entire conundrum.

"The honour of your presence" formally invites guests to a ceremony in a house of worship—note the British spelling of "honour." "The pleasure of your company" means the ceremony will take place in a secular location, such as a hotel or restaurant, or that the invitation is solely for the reception. The name of the place of worship is included, but not the address, which is detailed with directions on an enclosure.

In the traditional scenario, with the bride's parents hosting the wedding, the bride's name always precedes the groom's, and although "Mr." is used with the groom's name, the bride's name does not take "Miss" or "Ms." or her surname. If the groom's parents are hosting, this rule is reversed. Dads and grooms get to keep their professional titles ("Judge"; "Doctor"), moms and brides do not—unless the bride is issuing the invitation with her fiancé (as opposed to either of their parents), in which case she can use hers. Brides and grooms on active duty should use their military titles, and dads can use theirs even if retired.

DELPHINE AND HENRY'S INVITATION.
Paper: Orange Blossom, Sheer Celebration Laser Imprintable Invitations, Cardeaux. Computer fonts: Bembo; Adine Kernberg (first letter of bride/groom names).

CHRISTINE AND DAVID'S INVITATION.
Paper: Battenburg, Sheer Celebration Laser Imprintable Invitations, Cardeaux.

REBECCA AND DAVID'S INVITATION.
Paper: Butterflies, Sheer Celebration Laser Imprintable Invitations, Cardeaux. Computer font: Chanson d'Amour.

ISABELLA AND GRAHAM'S INVITATION by Patti Copenhaver. Rubber stamps: Romantic Rose and Letter #A1564E, Rubber Stampede. Other: gold pen, handmade paper.

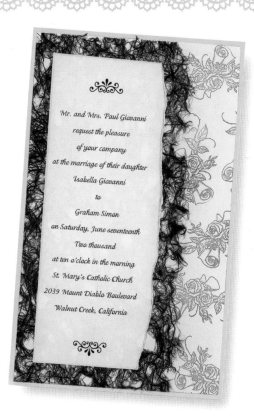

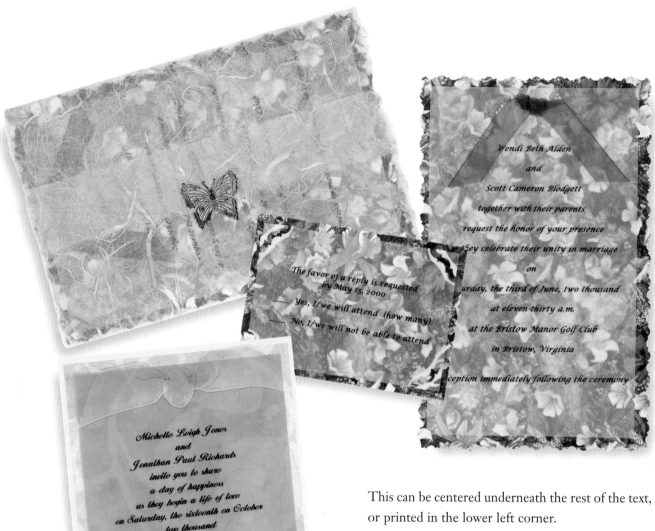

The favor of a reply is requested
by May 15, 2000

____ *Yes, I/we will attend (how many)* ____

____ *No, I/we will not be able to attend*

Wendi Beth Alden

and

Scott Cameron Blodgett

together with their parents

request the honor of your presence

...they celebrate their unity in marriage

on

...urday, the third of June, two thousand

at eleven-thirty a.m.

at the Bristow Manor Golf Club

in Bristow, Virginia

...ception immediately following the ceremony

Michelle Leigh Jones
and
Jonathan Paul Richards
invite you to share
a day of happiness
as they begin a life of love
on Saturday, the sixteenth on October
two thousand
at six o'clock in the evening
United Methodist Church
230 Park Avenue
Bayside, Ohio

The treatment of "RSVP"—an abbreviation of the French *répondez s'il vous plaît*—varies. For invitations to ceremonies only, it's rarely necessary, unless there's a chance the house of worship will be too small to accommodate all the guests. If you are asking for a reply, do so in one of several ways: "RSVP"; "kindly respond"; or "the favour of a reply is requested"—note the British spelling of "favour."

This can be centered underneath the rest of the text, or printed in the lower left corner.

Save your guests any potential embarrassment by specifying the dress code on the invitation. "Black tie" means men in tuxedos, women in gowns. To request formal attire without making tuxedos compulsory, state "black tie optional." Guests should be notified if the site requires certain informal dress or footwear, especially for an outdoor event: "Dress for a day at the beach."

Because rules are made to be broken, alternatives to formal wording include: dropping the "u" and using the American spellings of "honor" and "favor"; skipping "honor" altogether, and opting for the warmer "We cordially invite you"; using numerals for the year; or using professional titles for brides and mothers. At the end of the day, propriety aside, the wording should be consistent with the overall tone of the wedding.

And if you're the lucky bride who's having a small wedding, you can officially forget all of the above and invite your guests via handwritten note!

Envelopes

Although home computers can be used to print the rest of the invitation, there are some components of wedding stationery that etiquette enforcers insist must be handwritten. One is the thank-you note; the other is the envelope address. Even though it may be more efficient to print labels on adhesive paper, nobody wants to feel as if she's just another name on a database. If your list is topping the 500 mark and you fear the onset of premature arthritis, get your groom, bridesmaids, and parents to help.

Because many contemporary invitations are now trimmed in custom sizes, inner envelopes are becoming less common. But when mailing a double envelope, make sure that, for consistency, the same person addresses both. The return address of the hosts should be written on the back flap of the outer envelope. Finally, to state the obvious, address the envelopes before stuffing! Otherwise, the precious contents will be subjected to the pressure of the pen.

Sealing wax comes in an array of colors, but be forewarned that imprimaturs often get cracked in the mail. A sticker has a better chance of survival.

One of the most charming ways to decorate envelopes is to use postage stamps that reflect the theme of the wedding. Stamps today are available in so many designs that this is not difficult to do. Mail invites six to eight weeks before the wedding—ten weeks if mailing abroad. Don't forget to send one to the officiant, one to your parents, and—if you're wondering about how well your cherished missive will weather the postal system—yourself!

WENDI AND SCOTT by Wendi Beth Alden. Patterned paper: Paper Products.

MICHELLE AND JONATHAN'S INVITATION by Theresa Cifali. Leaf patterned paper: Colors by Design. Vellum: Paper Cuts. Premium cover: Marco's. Punch: rectangular, McGill. Computer font: John Hancock. Adhesive: ATG 700 Glue Tape. Organza ribbon.

SEALED WITH STYLE by Jenny Jackson. *Back envelope.* Paper: The Natural Paper Co. Wax: Freund-Mayer. Seal: Freund-Mayer. *Front envelope.* Paper: Hero Arts. Wax: Freund-Mayer. Stamp: D.O.T.S. Fun idea to note: Jenny imprinted the wax with the same stamp she used to decorate the paper inside.

Programs

FORGET THE FLOWERS, forget the cake. This is what it's all about: a commitment to love and honor come rain or come shine. That's why the ceremony program may be the most meaningful wedding keepsake. Through readings, scripture, poems, and music, it tells the story of a special union, of two becoming one. Admittedly, it can sometimes read like a theatrical playbill, with lines of dialogue and a list of supporting characters. After all, marriage is a dramatic event—there's even a rehearsal! And if the program is the official script, then timelines are the crib notes, directing players to their places throughout each act of the performance.

Program Components

A program can be as concise or descriptive as the couple desires. Some elements couples include are: a page thanking family and friends for their involvement; the names of the wedding party members, the couples' parents, the officiant, and any other readers or soloists, along with a few words about why these folks are VIPs; the ceremony, including liturgical texts, secular readings, and musical selections; and a paragraph in commemoration of deceased relatives. The back cover can be unadorned or decorated; it's a good place to note if flash photography is prohibited during the service.

Prelude
Solo-"Ave Maria"
Processional
Greeting & Prayer of Invocation
Wedding Message
Solo-"The Lord's Prayer"
Exchange of Vows & Rings
Blessing of the Marriage
Presentation of the Couple
Recessional
Toast to Lanae & Darry

A Celebration
of Love
Lanae & Darry
June 1, 1999
Little Theatre

In addition to covering those basics, the program is the ideal place to elaborate on the ceremony's religious and cultural rituals—from the *saptapadi*, or seven steps, of a Hindu union to the *sheva b'rachot*, or seven blessings, of a Jewish one. If the bride and groom come from different faiths, a paragraph can announce the positive aspects of pairing the two. If parts of the ceremony will be performed in a foreign language, the program can provide a translation and an explanation of specific ethnic traditions. Programs might also list the lyrics to a communal hymn or words to a congregational prayer. Include any information that will help guests to follow along and better understand the vows.

Check with your rabbi, priest, or justice of the peace: Depending on the nature of the ceremony—

PETAL PAPER PROGRAM by Jaime Echt/Crafter's Workshop. Paper: handmade dried rose petal paper, The Natural Paper Co. Punch: 1/8" hole, McGill. Adhesive: High Tack Xyron Machine. Ribbon: 1" sheer. Fun idea to note: Jaime first printed onto the vellum, fed it through the Xyron Machine, trimmed the vellum, and mounted it to the petal paper.

WHITE/WHITE PROGRAM by Jaime Echt/Crafter's Workshop. Paper: handmade skeleton leaf paper, The Natural Paper Co. Scissors: Paper trimmer by Fiskars. Punch: McGill. Ribbon: 5/8" sheer. Fun idea to note: Jaime printed the cover text onto vellum and trimmed it to size. She folded the handmade paper, placed the vellum on top, punched holes through the top two layers, and then slipped the folded insert inside.

GERALYN AND ANDREW by Becky Higgins. Pen: Zig Writer, EK Success. Pencil: Prismacolor, Sanford. Lettering, corners, leaf accent: "Wedding Alphabets" CD, *Creating Keepsakes*.

CELEBRATION OF LOVE by Lanae Johnson. Paper: Trellis Cachet, Paper Direct. Pen: Uniball Gel Impact, Sanford. Adhesive: Photo Mount, Creative Memories. Fun idea to note: This unusual program format is a great keepsake for guests to take home!

A Celebration of Love
Lanae & Darry
June 1, 1991
Little Theatre

Prelude
Solo - "Ave Maria"
Processional
Greeting & Prayer of Invocation
Wedding Message
Solo - "The Lord's Prayer"
Exchange of Vows & Rings
Blessing of the Marriage
Presentation of the Couple
Recessional
Toast to Lanae & Darry

Pastor Darrel Johnson: Darry's brother from Dallas
Matron of Honor: Lisa LaPage, Lanae's sister from Tucson
Best Man: Wade Gueddert, Darry's friend since childhood
Soloist: Preston Fry, Darry's friend
The Konchorde String Quartet

THE WEDDING OF

AMY & LANE

SEPTEMBER 4, 1994
LAS VEGAS, NEVADA

TODAY BEGINS OUR MARRIED LIFE,
FROM THIS DAY ON AS MAN & WIFE.

civil or religious, traditional or non—you may be able to incorporate your own vows. And even if you get the OK, proceed with caution. Writing your own vows is an awesome responsibility! To help you and your intended rise to the occasion, start a notebook or journal—separate or shared—and jot down scraps of conversations, songs, and movie scenes that melt your heart. Think back to bedtime stories, ethnic folktales, or favorite poems that best express your feelings about love. Fill a page with words describing your fiancé—how you met, the moment you knew he was "the one"—and your hopes for the future. Refer to the dictionary for fundamental definitions of "faithfulness," "commitment," and "trust." Scratch out your sample pledges apart from each other, then compare notes and fine-tune together (otherwise you may be in for some surpris-

ing declarations on your wedding day). Based on the length, and your comfort level, pen or print the final version on handsome paper. And unless your gown is so contemporary that it comes equipped with cargo pockets, entrust the documents to the maid of honor and best man. Afterward, for posterity, frame the two papers side by side. But don't discard the rough drafts! Along with the notebook, they'll become sentimental touchstones—the earliest recorded evidence of your partnership. On anniversaries (or whenever you hit a rough patch), pull them out for review.

Programs printed on similar paper and in a similar style as the invitation present a seamless look, so continue the color palette and symbolic motif established with stationery. Use decorative fonts for titles, but set large passages of text in an easy-to-read typeface. The program cover is an appropriate showcase for an artful photograph (*Winter Wonderland, below*) or symbolic line drawing (*Wedding of Amy & Lane, opposite*), and witnesses at a small wedding will cherish an original watercolor illustration. To represent friendship, love, and loyalty, Irish-Americans may feature a motif of the hands, heart, and crown of the traditional *Claddagh* ring; those with an Indian heritage can border pages with ornate paisley patterns that customarily are painted in henna on the hands and feet of the bride.

A CELEBRATION OF LOVE by Lanae Johnson. Adhesive: glue pen. Fun idea to note: Lanae repeated the LOVE design elements of her wedding invitation on this program. See other elements from Lanae's wedding on pages 24 and 86.

THE WEDDING OF AMY & LANE PROGRAM by Lanae Johnson. Fun idea to note: Lanae printed this booklet-style program and then mounted its back page onto cardstock that she had trimmed to be slightly larger than the size of the program. This gave the program added weight and interest. You could choose a cardstock color that coordinates with the wedding colors to dress up any simple printed program.

WINTER WONDERLAND by Cathy Arnold. Punch: small hole. Computer font: CAC Leslie. Ribbon. See other elements of the wedding Cathy planned with her daughter on pages 23 and 42.

Intensify color for an invigorating effect: A printed vellum cover in pale lavender punctuated by a deep purple ribbon along the papers' crease would look streamlined yet rich. Color also holds symbolic meaning in many cultures. For instance, Chinese-Americans may accent their programs with red, which stands for joy and luck. Loop satin, raffia, and organza ribbons through a couple of hole punches near the program's fold (*Petal Paper Program, page 30*). Tasseled cords in longer programs can be used by guests to bookmark passages during the ceremony.

Because quality paper folded in half is all it takes to create program booklets, it's quite easy to

design and print materials on personal computer systems. Depending on the size of the guest list, either pace yourself and print the lot or make multiple copies of a clean version. Assembling programs is a great group activity—get bridesmaids and groomsmen together for the task. Aim to have the programs ready as soon as all the elements of the ceremony are confirmed—at least a month in advance—and remember to print many extras. Anybody who gets a special mention in the program will want to take a clean copy home as a keepsake.

At the ceremony site, stack programs in eye-catching baskets by the entry, or arrange for a member of the wedding party to distribute them. This job usually falls to ushers, who are seating guests.

Timelines

The ceremony is the main event, but weddings these days seem to last entire weekends! Timelines are indispensable tools that tell all the participants exactly what they're expected to do, exactly when they're expected to do it.

Because timelines can (and should) be meticulously detailed, plain old word processed pages with crucial instructions highlighted in boldface are clear and to the point—although a cover sheet featuring the motif does polish the presentation (*Love Itinerary, opposite*). Consider creating a series of schedules. A master list could break down, minute by minute, every single step from the rehearsal through the departure for the airport. Comprehensive outlines would include: a mini-phone book listing the names, roles, addresses, cell, fax, e-mail, and beeper numbers of all involved—not just the maid of honor and the best man, but also the photographer, makeup artist, banquet manager, and bandleader; arrival times; estimated times for every activity, from the walk down the aisle to the opening toast to the bouquet toss; directions to the ceremony and reception sites; and a separate sheet concerning transportation information. The more precise the agenda, the less likely Murphy's Law will result. An abridged version, focusing exclusively on the ceremony, could be distributed at the rehearsal (and it pays to ask a bridesmaid to bring extras on the day itself—somebody always forgets). Other custom-tailored checklists could cover such sub-topics as honeymoon travel (don't forget to renew your passport!) and the specific responsibilities of attendants. For example, does the best man know he's in charge of reimbursing the officiant?

Regimented itineraries are essential for the key players, but cheerfully illustrated sheets are a more festive way to inform family and friends of the various gatherings that will occur over the course of several days—or weeks, if counting backward to bachelor parties and bridal showers. Establish a few bright icons to indicate time and place (*opposite*), and modify the page for the rehearsal dinner, bridesmaids' luncheon, and post-reception brunch. ✍

WEDDING WEEKEND SURVIVAL GUIDE by Lanae Johnson. Paper: Mara Mi. Die cuts: Mara Mi. Pen: Micron Pigma, Sakura. Lettering: Funky, *The Journaling Genie* #3. Adhesive: Sailor glue pen. Fun idea to note: Lanae chose scrapbook supplies that correlated with specific events to convey an upbeat tone. This creates a great visual memento of the weekend!

LOVE ITINERARY by Lanae Johnson. Fun idea to note: Lanae typed the itinerary, made as many copies as she needed, and then adhered them to cardstock.

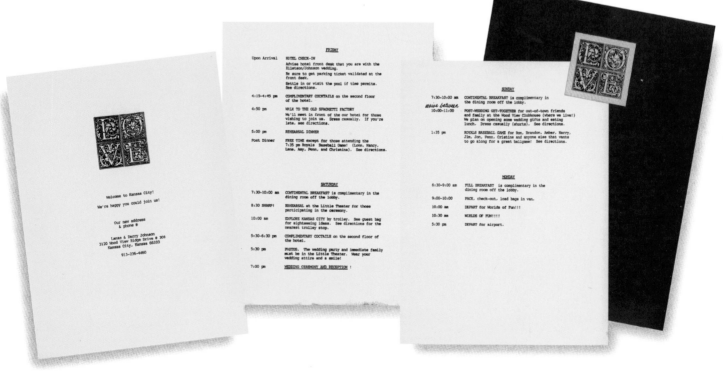

Photography

YOU'VE PROBABLY hired a pro. Maybe, like more and more brides these days, you've hired two: one for formal portraits, the other for photojournalistic action shots. You're armed both with your list of must-have images *(see Wedding Photo Checklist)*, and have assigned a pal to tag along and discreetly point out VIPs—guests you definitely want captured on film. But no matter how perfect the professional photography, it's often the spontaneous snapshots taken by friends that end up being the most fun. And everybody's an amateur shutterbug. So if Uncle Harry offers to videotape the event, or Cousin Elaine insists on shooting a few roles, graciously accept and gently suggest they adhere to the following advice.

Know Your Camera

There's a reason cameras come with manuals. Read them! Get familiar with your unit's special features before the big event. Standard small-format, point-and-click, 35mm cameras are best for photos that will not be enlarged beyond 8 x 10 inches—past that point, they begin to lose their sharpness. Medium-format, or 2¼, cameras, which use slightly bigger film, are better for formal portraits because prints retain their clarity when blown up. Digital cameras make it easy to transfer images to disk or CD-ROM as an alternative to storing negatives. Scans can be color-corrected on computer—and posted on the internet as an online wedding album.

A film speed of 100–200 is fine for photos taken in broad daylight or well-lit indoor spaces, with or without flash. For darker interiors, such as the inside of a church or a candle-illuminated ballroom, speeds of 400 and up are more light-sensitive. (Note that some houses of worship place restrictions on photography, forbidding flashes, for example, or limiting access to sacred areas: Check with your officiant.) Certain films, such as Kodak Max, are specifically made to capture action in inclement weather. And for a wild, otherworldly look, infrared, a black-and-white film that reads heat instead of light, provides high-contrast outdoor photos.

Different lens adaptations allow for out-of-the-ordinary shots. Many automatics come equipped with zoom and panoramic features: a zoom lens enables the photographer to frame close-ups from a distance, and thereby capture candid moments without being intrusive; a wide-angle lens produces a horizontal image that encompasses a broad expanse—a panorama. Portraits shot in soft focus give the subjects a pleasingly hazy glow and reduce the appearance of wrinkles. Experiment with a fish-eye lens for a funhouse, peephole effect.

Photos by Brenda Bennett. Fun idea to note: Brenda isn't afraid to get close with her camera. A zoom lens can help you achieve the look of closeness without you having to stand very near; sometimes it's better if the bride and groom, or whomever you see through your lens, aren't aware that they are being photographed at that moment.

Lighting

"In my experience," states Matt Mendelsohn, photo editor for *USA Today*, "amateur photographers make two major mistakes. First, they don't get close enough. Move into your subject for maximum impact. Second, they shoot in direct sunlight. Look for shaded, softer, dappled light. It eliminates harsh shadows the sun casts on faces." Photographers refer to this kind of natural light as "open shade" *(opposite and above)*. It's an evocative option, since it captures the shifting nuances of the daylight. But because it can be fleeting,

outdoor photographs may benefit from the support of a flash. The flash allows the photographer to shoot in available light without having to rely on a meter to adjust the exposure per picture. When shooting indoors, however, in order to light both subjects and their backgrounds, a flash must be used with additional light sources, such as strobes, situated around the room and set to go off simultaneously.

The best way to avoid the dreaded red-eye syndrome is to raise the flash higher than the camera: Most automatics don't offer this option, although many come equipped with a pre-flash that reduces the effect. After the fact, a red-eye remover pen can conceal the glaring dots on the prints *(see Resources)*.

Umbrella lighting—set on tripods and shaded by black umbrellas—produces softer-than-flash lighting for formal group portraits. And for portraits taken

in a house of worship that forbids flash photography, time exposure requires that the subjects remain perfectly still as the camera, steadied on a tripod, slowly exposes the film. Any movement will blur the image.

Color vs. Black-and-White

Why choose? Color conveys the vibrancy, the immediacy, the rainbow glory of the day. It records all the fabulous shades of your expertly coordinated place cards and tablecloths, bridesmaid dresses and bouquets. Black-and-white imbues photos with a classic quality. (It also minimizes blemishes and other minor flaws.) Ask one of your nonprofessional photographers to carry two cameras, like professionals do, each loaded with a different type of film. To give your portraits a lovely antique feeling, print a few in sepia tones *(above and opposite)*. Most processing labs offer this as an alternative to traditional, black-and-white (in essence, it's brown-and-white).

Creative Uses of Photography

Photographs don't only have to document your wedding: They can decorate it, too. One special way to acknowledge that your marriage is the latest in a long line of illustrious family mergers is to display other wedding portraits—of grandparents, parents, beloved uncles and aunts, hitched siblings and kissing cousins—each individually framed and clustered together atop a small table at the reception site. It's a grateful gesture, a tip of the hat to the generations before you, and it will give older relatives an awful lot to reminisce about.

You can also create displays with photos of friends. Add an enclosure to the invitation asking guests to send a shot of themselves with the bride, groom, or both. Reproduced at a standard size, such as 8 x 10", these images can line a hall at a home reception or border the wall at a garden party. Another sweet variation on this theme: Show the bride, groom, and members of the wedding as children.

Laurie Elizabeth English and Kersten Rolf Flurer started their new life together with a sense of humor and some playful photos. The duo's favorite movie is the Bogart-Bergman classic, *Casablanca*. By happy coincidence, bride and groom were each able to fit into period clothes saved by the mother of the bride. Dressed like their silver-screen idols, the couple posed in front of a forties fighter jet at a nearby air base, then printed their invitation with the images.

Guests at a small wedding will relish a slide show during which you and your groom affectionately describe what each person pictured has meant to you, or a funny home video spoofing all the infamous foibles of your courtship. At the reception, designate a well-lit corner as a mini-studio (like at the prom). Use a white sheet as a backdrop, rent a few umbrella lights if necessary, then encourage

Photos by Brenda Bennett. Fun idea to note: Brenda tries to face her subjects away from the sun. If their faces are shaded, she uses a flash to help brighten up the photo. By steadying herself, she can hold her camera still for crisp pictures. And before pressing the camera's shutter, she scans all four corners in the viewfinder to make sure there are no unwanted items in her picture.

bows.) Number each camera according to table number, and ask a friend to round them all up by the end of the evening. After the rolls are developed, arrange the shots into small albums, keyed to the number of each table.

Preserving Photos and Videos

Color images are composed of organic dyes that fade when exposed to light (both fluorescent and natural), heat, and humidity. Today, it's also common for labs to produce black-and-white images through a color process (as opposed to true black-and-whites, which are printed from silver with gelatin); these fade as fast as any other color print. To slow the aging process, store negatives and prints separately (that way, if one set is accidentally damaged, the second's still safe) in polyethylene plastic sleeves or acid- and lignin-free paper envelopes or boxes. These protect photos from light and pollutants without depriving them of air (see *Keepsake Boxes*). Keep photos dry, in the dark, at a temperature of about 65 degrees Fahrenheit. Handle images with care: Natural skin oils deteriorate a photo's emulsion, so keep hands clean, and only touch the edges of prints (conservationists actually wear white cotton gloves). According to studies by the Smithsonian Institution, freezing negatives helps them last up to 500 times longer. One company, Metal Edge, offers refrigerator kits for this purpose (see *Resources*). Alternately, scan photos onto your hard drive and back them up on CD-ROM—digital images can be retouched at any time. Videos should be stored upright in their cases, away from electronic and magnetic equipment, which fade the film. And remove the clip at the back, so that nobody accidentally records the Super Bowl over your big day. ✍

assorted groupings of guests—fraternity brothers, four generations of women, all the little rascals under the age of 10—to pose for Polaroids. You may like to take a handful along on your honeymoon, just for fun. Later, enclose copies with thank-you notes; they're guaranteed to be a hit.

Many couples today opt to place flash-equipped disposable cameras throughout the reception room. They can be a great way for strangers seated at the same table to break the ice, and sometimes they provide a serendipitous shot or two. (Note that disposables specially decorated for weddings often contain only 12 shots, while those in regular packaging usually offer twice as many for the same price. You could decorate these yourself with stickers or

CASABLANCA INVITATION by Jeanne English. Paper: Hammermill Cover (white). Vellum: Gil Clear, Gilbert. Computer font: Papyrus, Letra Set. Adhesive: ATG tape.

FOUR SQUARE PHOTOS PAGE by Megan McMurdie. Fun idea to note: Megan balanced this page by placing the photos of herself and her new husband in opposite corners.

DAISY PAGE by Megan McMurdie. Copper paper: AccuCut. Daisy die cuts: My Mind's Eye. Pen: Zig Writer, EK Success. Fun idea to note: Megan replaced the yellow centers of the daisies with copper paper to coordinate with the border around the pictures.

UNDER THE TREES PAGE by Megan McMurdie. Vellum paper: Paper Co. Pen: Gelly Roll.

Table Decorations

SWEET THINGS come in small packages. Although the bride's most exciting moment of the day may be the smooch at the altar, guests get a little thrill when they approach their table, where place cards position them boy-girl-boy-girl and intriguing paper boxes beg to be opened. Because items such as imprinted napkins, menus, and centerpiece petals are often taken home and pressed into scrapbooks, attention to detail does make a difference. Thank guests for sharing in your celebration by giving table decorations the TLC they deserve.

Place Cards

The distinctions have been blurred over time, but technically, escort cards—arranged alphabetically on a designated table near the dining room entrance—notify guests of their table number, while place cards—listing the name only, and laid on the assigned table, either atop the plate or at the "12 o'clock" spot above the setting—tell them exactly where to sit. Escort cards serve a practical purpose and have a romantic history: In Edwardian days, instead of numbers, they bore the name of the lady each gen-

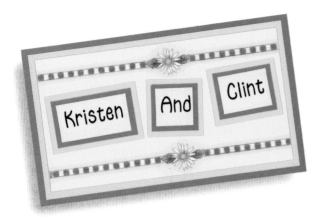

EMBOSSED PLACE SETTING by Jenny Jackson. Template: Lasting Impressions for Paper, Inc. Computer font: CK Script, "Best of Creative Lettering" CD Vol. 1, *Creating Keepsakes*. Ribbon: Offray.

WINTER WEDDING PLACE SETTING by Cathy Arnold. *Place Card.* Template: "Snowflake," Lasting Impressions. Computer font: CAC Leslie. Adhesive: glue pen. Other: miniature silk roses. *Rice cone* (see page 55). *Advice card.* Computer font: CAC Leslie. *Cocoa sachets.* Template: "Snowflake," Lasting Impressions. Computer font: CAC Leslie. Fun idea to note: Cathy dry embossed snowflakes onto cardstock then cut the paper to make the flapped envelope, then stapled on the ribbon and pinecones.

KRISTEN AND CLINT by Joy Macdonnell/ My Scrapbook Store. Label for guest basket (see PICNIC WEDDING, below).

PICNIC WEDDING by Joy Mcdonnell. Basket: Total Crafts. Paper: DMD Industries; Paper Adventures. Stickers: Me & My BIG Ideas. Computer font: Color Me 8, "Lettering Delights" CD, *Inspire Graphics*. Fun idea to note: Upon arriving at an outdoor wedding reception on a grassy hillside, guests received a picnic basket filled with a large tablecloth and a delicious picnic meal!

tleman would accompany to dinner. (Perhaps seating plans have replaced this custom, since receptions are now notorious opportunities for mischievous matchmaking on the part of the bride and groom!)

At formal events, a small unsealed envelope addressed to the guest contains a card indicating the table number, and the note is propped up on its open flap. In addition to the elegance of this display, it also offers convenience: Materials can be printed well before seating is finalized, and cards switched at the last minute to accommodate musical chairs. Less formal receptions may feature horizontally folded, or tented, escort cards, with names on the outside front cover and numbers on the inside back. The absence of an envelope gives tent cards a breezy, modern feeling, although lettering, embossing, and other embellishments can considerably glam them up.

As with invitations, escort and place cards can become miniature paper minefields thanks to the etiquette of titles. "Mr. and Mrs. Frederick Smith" is the traditional mode of address for a married couple, but "Henrietta and Frederick Smith" gives a wife equal billing and sidesteps sticky issues of professional (doctor, lawyer, army officer) accreditations. In the formal "Mr. and Mrs." address, it's customary to use the husband's first name, and this also helps to avoid confusion at a family affair where indubitably there will be more than one couple by the surname of "Smith"; without the titles, however, the wife's name ("Henrietta") should precede the husband's ("and Frederick Smith"). It gets more complicated: Unmarried couples and married couples with different last names should be addressed on two separate lines, with the woman on top ("Henrietta Foster/Frederick Smith"); if using titles, she is referred to as "Ms." Although it might make life a little easier to mark escort cards for single friends "Mr. Frederick Smith and Guest," it's not terribly welcoming. Whenever possible, find out the full name of the mystery date. Unescorted women can be addressed with ("Ms. Henrietta Foster") or without ("Henrietta Foster") a title, and single women of any age can be addressed as "Miss," although the term is usually reserved for girls under 13. Boys of the same age are formally referred to as "Master," but it is always appropriate to omit titles from children's names. Be consistent: If female guests won't have titles, then "Mr. Smith" should not be coming to dinner. Got all that?

Compared to the rules of address, designing escort and place cards can be a strictly creative endeavor. To craft unique cards, combine scheme, theme, and season. Standard black-on-white is always the starting point, but, because they're quite small, cards can sustain a shot of strong color.

Customize plain cards with embossed borders, stamped symbols, pressed sprigs, or ribbon threaded through a hole punch (*Christine Cain Place Card, opposite*). Mat hand-lettered nameplates on colored backdrops (*Adam Fulton Place Card* and *Melanie Place Card, page 46*), or overlay solid papers with lace or vellum (*Kelly McDonald Place Card; Mr. Ryan O'Connelly, opposite*). Deckled edges can effectively eliminate the fuzzy perforations of computer sheets. Grace a tented card with a crystal bead threaded on embroidery floss that matches the ink color (slide the string's knot underneath the paper's fold).

In fact, according to the formality of the affair, place cards hardly have to be cards at all. Celebrate autumn's cornucopia by scripting names on tiny gourds and pumpkins. For a winter wedding, cards can be inserted into unadorned snow globes or propped atop a bed of pine needles. At a casual springtime garden party, print cards on a hodgepodge of patterned papers that mimic the cheerful ginghams and plaids of country linens, then clip with mini-clothespins to a clothesline near the entrance. Or garnish painterly floral paper with a bouquet of punched daisies (*Jen Jacobson Place Card, opposite*).

Kids and adults alike will be enchanted by pinwheel place cards at an oceanside ceremony: Use a 5-inch square of heavyweight paper, leave a space about the size of a quarter in the center, then cut from the four corners to the edge of this inner circle to make four triangles. Above the right-hand edge of the top triangle, write the name of a guest, then fold the left corner in to the center circle. Fold in the left corners of the remaining three triangles and secure with an enameled marking tack through the circle and into a three-foot-high quarter-inch dowel. Label the tack with a numbered sticker indicating the table, and plant in the sand!

CHRISTINE CAIN PLACE CARD. Card: Battenburg (white), Sheer Celebration by Cardeaux.

KELLY MCDONALD TENT CARD by Susana Espinosa. Punch: small hole. Rubber stamps: Romantic Rose, Rubber Stampede. Pens/Pencils: watercolors. Stickers: gold photo corners. Embossing: inkpad by Rubber Stampede; gold powder. Scissors: straight and decorative edged. Adhesive: glue stick. Other: thin gold cording; gold heart charm. Fun idea to note: Susana cut cream paper and patterned vellum into a 7" x 5$\frac{1}{2}$" rectangle and folded both in half. She embossed a rose onto the front half of the vellum and colored it with the watercolors. She used a computer to print the guest's name on cardstock and trimmed this with the decorative edged scissors. Susana created a burgundy border for the name sheet, and used photo corners to adhere this to the front of the embossed vellum. To finish, she layered the cream and vellum cards, threaded cording through the fold, and tied on a gold charm.

MR. RYAN O'CONNELLY PLACE CARD by Jaime Echt. Paper: Paper Complements Papers; handmade skeleton leaf paper, The Natural Paper Co. Scissors: paper trimmer by Fiskars. Adhesive: Xyron High Tack Machine. Ribbon: 3/8" sheer. Fun idea to note: Jaime printed the guests' names on vellum, and she cut it and the handmade paper to size. She fed these sheets through the Xyron Machine. She secured 6" of ribbon to the ribbed paper by sticking it to the handmade paper; she then stuck these sheets to the vellum.

JEN JACOBSON PLACE CARD by Jenny Jackson. Rice paper: Freund-Mayer. Daisy punch: Family Treasures. Computer font: CK Calligraphy, "Best of Creative Lettering" CD Vol 1, *Creating Keepsakes*.

MR. BENJAMIN ECHT PLACE CARD by
Jaime Echt. Paper: Paper Complements.
Scissors: paper trimmer by Fiskars. Computer
font: Inda S Caps. Adhesive: glue stick that
dries clear; double-sided mounting tape.
Other: scoring blade for paper trimmer or
bone folder and ruler. Fun idea to note: Jaime
first cut, scored, and folded the ribbed paper
into the place card shape. Then she printed
the name onto vellum. Using the glue stick,
she attached it to the paper.

ADAM FULTON PLACE CARD by Becky
Higgins. Pencils: Prismacolor, Sanford.
Computer font, border: "Wedding Alphabets"
CD, *Creating Keepsakes*.

MS. ELIZABETH MYERS PLACE CARD by
Jaime Echt. Paper: handmade skeleton leaf
paper, The Natural Paper Co. Scissors: scallop scissors by Family Treasures; paper
trimmer by Fiskars. Adhesive: glue stick. Fun
idea to note: When Jaime printed the name
onto vellum, she left enough room at the top
so that it could be folded over the handmade
paper. She trimmed the bottom of the vellum
with the scallop scissors so that it would be
shorter than the paper.

MELANIE PLACE CARD by Becky Higgins.
Pencils: Prismacolor, Sanford. Chalk: Craf-T
Products. Computer font, border: "Wedding
Alphabets" CD, *Creating Keepsakes*.

WEDDING PARTY PLACE CARDS by Kelly
Edgerton. Paper: Pebbles in My Pocket.
Vellum: Making Memories. Punch: 1/16" hole,
Marvy Uchida. Computer font: CK
Contemporary, "Wedding Alphabets" CD,
Creating Keepsakes. Other: DMC embroidery
floss. Fun idea to note: For her lettering, Kelly
chose the color blue for fill pattern 1 and light
purple for fill pattern 2.

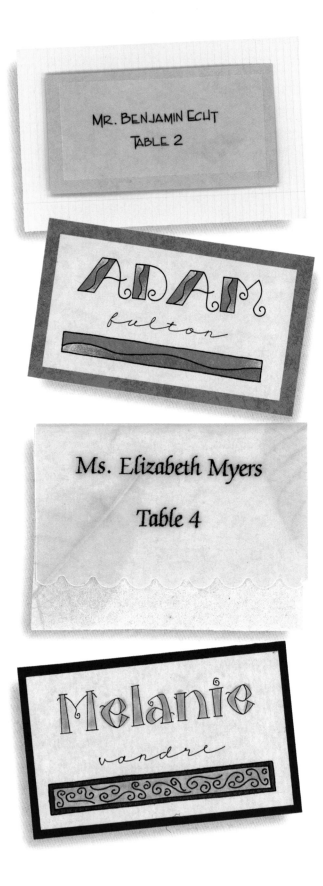

Colorful paper umbrellas festooned with thin paper flags "flying" the guest's name make festive seating cards at a tropical-themed party. Or stencil seasonal motifs—of sunbursts, maple leaves, snowflakes—on card stock, cut out, snip a small V-shaped notch into each paper ornament and, after adding the name, slip the notch over the rim of a water glass to secure.

The Table

Centerpieces may catch the eye, but memorable tables are built from the bottom up. Before the salad fork and the fish knife take their respective places beside the plate, grace the tablecloth with a paper runner bordered by a handwritten poem:

"O love is the crooked thing, there is nobody wise enough to find out all that is in it . . ." (W. B. Yeats). Then dust the surface with confetti shaped to capture the theme.

Depending on choices made for the meal, each place setting could contain as many as four glasses (water, white and red wine, champagne), two spoons (soup and dessert), four knives (fish, dinner, steak, butter), and four forks (salad, fish, dinner, dessert)—plus a stack of plates and a bowl for broth. To counterbalance all this cutlery, cluster votives toward the center of the table. Wrapped in tinted, translucent rice paper, these small candles instantly make the atmosphere more intimate. They're also precious—and low calorie!—party

favors. (Luminarias—votives nestled in sand inside plain brown lunch bags—evocatively illuminate outdoor pathways. Use punches to cut patterns in the paper for the light to dance through.)

With so many handsome papers to choose from, there's no excuse for ungainly metal table number stands. Horizontally folded cards can echo the design of escort cards; flea market frames turn painted numbers into works of art; and die-cuts shaped like leaves and attached with floral wire to false stems can be nestled among the centerpiece's blossoms. Spelled-out numbers ("Table One") have a formal impact which can be slightly softened with lowercase letters ("table one"). For small or specially shaped cards, the numeral alone is refreshingly concise ("1"). And at an informal reception, the interesting outlines of numerals lend themselves to amusingly childlike illustrations—imagine the triangular sail of a "4," for example, and the bobbing balloon of a "9." Or forget about digits altogether, and name tables after favorite flowers, cities, movies, or dances. Wouldn't you rather be seated at the "Tango" table?

The ordinary linen napkin is the dining room equivalent of the little black dress: Add just the right accessory, and it's the easiest way to decorate a setting. Rolled into a column, it can hold breadsticks, aromatic herbs such as lavender or rosemary, a single-stemmed blossom, a handmade bookmark, a scroll containing the lyrics to a cherished love song, or even a place card—tucked like a ticket into the fabric's folds. Continuing the stationery themes of the escort, place, and table cards, wispy mulberry, petal, or patterned paper links can ring the gathered linen (*Embossed Place Setting, page 42*). For a medieval effect, bind the napkin with golden strands, then gather the ends on top of a square of heavy card stock and seal with a wax imprimatur. Or

LABELED BOTTLE by Lanae Johnson. Paper: Paper Pizazz, Hot Off the Press. Frame sticker: Frances Meyer. Pen: Micron Pigma, Sakura. Other: small bottles. Fun idea to note: Lanae used a color copier to reduce the photo to fit the sticker frame and chose border colors that coordinated with colors in the photo.

CHATEAU DE ELLETSON LABEL by Lanae Johnson. Paper: Paper Pizazz, Hot Off the Press. Banner and frame stickers: Frances Meyer. Pen: Micron Pigma, Sakura.

MAISON DE ELLETSON by Lanae Johnson. Photo frame card: Kolo. Banner sticker: Provo Craft. Pen: Micron Pigma, Sakura.

MAISON DE JOHNSONS LABEL by Lanae Johnson. Paper: Paper Pizazz, Hot Off the Press. Frame sticker: Frances Meyer. Pen: Micron Pigma, Sakura.

HUGS AND KISSES by Kesley Anderson/My Scrapbook Store. Paper: Paper Adventures; Cut it Up; DMD. Computer font: CK Wedding, "Best of Creative Lettering" CD Vol 2, *Creating Keepsakes*. Other: spoons, netting.

WEDDING BROOM by The Broom Lady, Richmond, VA. Parchment paper. Other: ribbon; miniature wedding rings; miniature brooms. Fun idea to note: Write the bride and groom's name on top left corner of the parchment paper, then write the message on the opposite side.

ORIGAMI STAR BOXES by The Broom Lady, Richmond, VA. Paper: 8 x 8-inch square. Fun idea to note: Print the phrase "Thank You," "Happy to See You," "Thanks for Coming," or the like, repeatedly onto one side of the paper. On the other, print the bride and groom's names. Photocopy and cut down to make square origami paper. (*See Origami Star Box directions, page 113.*)

if the size is right, tie the favor to the napkin with a gauzy organza ribbon.

Menus are a popular wedding souvenir, so place one per setting, on top of the plate. And when space is at a premium, menus can double as place cards. Print the guest's name at the top of the page, followed by the couple's names or monogram, the location, and the date. For a cohesive look, the menu stationery should match the invitation and place card, but at a casual gathering, it can be a separate keepsake, trimmed according to the wedding's theme—a couple getting married on the Cape might print the menu down the length of a lighthouse. Most stationery shops carry decoratively bordered cards made for laser printers.

Give a disposable camera to each table and encourage guests to use it *(page 53)*! For the newly-weds, the reception often becomes a blur of toasts and tosses and hurried reunions with out-of-town relatives. Amateur snapshots provide a window on just what was happening over at table eight all night long, and some surprisingly good candids may end up claiming a special place in scrapbooks, illustrating a keepsake guest book, or accompanying a thank-you note.

The bride and groom are queen and king for a day, so it's only fitting that they sit on temporary thrones. Letter the titles of wedding party members in colors that complement the reception space, then string signs from the backs of ballroom chairs at the bridal table *(Place Cards, page 47)*. Or script initials, first names, even "His" and "Hers" or "The Mr." and "The Mrs." on two squares of card stock, veil with a scrim of vellum, hole-punch the upper corners, and tie to the chair ribs with ribbons. Treat-filled favor boxes name-tagged with place cards can also be looped from chair backs.

Finally, don't forget the wee ones at a reception. Seat children at a separate table covered with butcher squares and bestow each place setting with an arts-and-crafts activity bag containing crayons, stickers, and comic books. The catering staff can

PYRAMID BOX by Diane Hackley. Template: pyramid box by Inkadinkado. Scissors: Fiskars. Wedding bells stamp: Embossing Arts Co. Small rose stamp: PrintWorks. Adhesive: Wonder Tape. Other: sheer ribbon; silver rings; paper flower by Modern Romance; Encore Metallics inkpad. Fun idea to note: Diane stamped the wedding bells on each triangle of the unfolded box.

PINWHEEL BOX by Diane Hackley. Template: pinwheel box by Inkadinkado. Word stamp: Hero Arts. Adhesive: Wonder Tape. Scissors: Fiskars. Ribbon: Offray. Other: Colorbox cat's eyes; Colorbox Metalextra; paper roses by Modern Romance.

TAKE-OUT FAVOR BOX by Diane Hackley. Fun idea to note: Many wedding guests will recognize the shape of this box—Chinese take-out! Diane adorned this box with festive wedding elements and topped it with a sheer ribbon.

change the squares with each course and set aside the kids' scribbles. By the end of the evening, the junior Picassos probably will have colored at least a couple of cute cartoon drawings.

Favors

For good luck, Japanese couples fold 1,001 origami cranes—birds that mate for life—and scatter the faithful paper fowl across the tables at their reception. The custom of presenting guests with sugared almonds, a symbol of fertility, can be traced back to ancient Rome. It's not necessary to give out favors, but—especially knowing it's going to take months to write all those thank-you notes—what better way to say, on the spot, "We're so happy you're here"?

A handmade touch can transform the most humble offerings into heartfelt gifts. Sweets are a standard favor, but personalize them: Bake and frost gingerbread brides, grooms, tiered cakes, and dia-

mond rings, then design a recipe card with a creative font and include it with the cookie box. Or cap homemade preserves with patterned fabric squares, trimmed at the edges with pinking shears and tied around the lid with metallic twine, then add a customized label that includes names, the place, and the date. If yours is a vintage year for a wedding, commemorate it with a label that depicts your imaginary *maison (page 48)*.

Better for waistlines than a box of chocolates, plants have become popular party fare. Tag seed packets, burlap sachets of bulbs, bundles of herbs, or terra-cotta potted shrubs with a card explaining how to care for (or cook) them. Emphasize the organic theme by peppering the paper with pressed leaves.

If you and your beloved are literary types, create a bookmark that features a reading from your ceremony. Acknowledge your heritage by sending guests home with a symbolic item, such as the

HEARTS BOXES by Lanae Johnson. Handmade paper. Pen: Micron Pigma, Sakura. Heart favors: The Natural Paper Co. Fun idea to note: Using the bride and groom's names makes for a thoughtful wedding memento, or you could personalize these favors with your guests names.

PYRAMID BOXES by Jaime Echt/Crafters Workshop. Die cut: Ellison #7 pyramid box. Ribbed paper: Cinnamon red, Paper Complements. Stamp: Francis Meyer. Other: sheer ribbon, heavy weight vellum. Fun idea to note: Jaime used 10" of ribbon to attach the name card. Coordinate paper and ribbon colors with the wedding colors.

STAND-UP CAMERA DIRECTIONS by Lanae Johnson. Tall table tent: Paper Direct. Pen: Micron Pigma, Sakura. Fun idea to note: These tall directions can't be missed by wedding guests!

CAMERA INSTRUCTIONS by Cathy Arnold. Fun idea to note: Cathy composed this poem to remind guests to use the disposable cameras and then leave them for the bride and groom. She cleverly surrounded her poem with a border that looks like camera film!

ROSE CAMERA TAG by Kelly Edgerton. Paper: Pebbles in My Pocket. Computer font: CK Roses, "Wedding Alphabet" CD, *Creating Keepsakes*. Stickers: "Red Roses Border Set," PrintWorks Studio Collection. Hole punch: Family Treasures. Ribbon: Offray. Fun idea to note: You could place these tags on each camera, which is a great reminder to guests to not take the camera home with them.

Here is a camera
Please use it a lot,
To take pictures of
What the photographer will not.

The flash is required
Because it is night.
If you don't use it,
The snaps won't come out right.

Pull out the front flap
to activate the flash.
You're all ready now.
So please snap, snap, snap!

The perfect distance
Is four to ten feet.
Any nearer or farther
Will be your defeat.

At the end of the evening
With all film exposed,
Put the camera in the basket...
We'll develop the photos.

You've helped to make our day special
Complete with love and laughter.
Thank you all so very much
For the memories you did capture!

Friends & Family,

Please use the camera provided on your table to capture the spirit of the evening. Your candid photographs will be added to the wedding scrapbook.

Enjoy yourselves, take lots of pictures, & make sure to leave the camera on the table.

Thank you.

I'm your camera
so have some fun,
You'll make our album
a special one!
Snap away as best
as you're able,
Then drop me off
at the gift table.

African-American broom, accompanied by an illuminated scroll explaining the custom (*page 49, center*). For a holiday wedding, craft paper pine tree ornaments. Whatever the token—a custom CD of favorite tracks, a stack of homemade glycerine soaps, a framed portrait—the wrapping is half the fun. Drop chocolate kisses into tulle totes that expose their foil wrappings, tie with a gold-bordered bow, and tag with a gold-embossed card (*Hugs and Kisses, page 49, top*). Cover a computer-printed sheet with affectionate phrases, then fold into a four-pointed box (*Origami Star Boxes, page 49, bottom*). Top boxes with paper roses and gilt baubles that entrepreneurial teen cousins may recycle into pendants and earrings (*page 50*). Or stamp Chinese take-out cartons with bells, bouquets, bubbly, and other marriage motifs (*page 51*). Whether dropping petal-paper sweetheart boxes on bread plates or piling crimson paper pyramids in a basket beside the door (*page 52*), to be plucked by their satin bows as guests make their exit, be sure to set aside a couple of the tiny treasures for yourselves.

Tosses

The toss is another centuries-old tradition, an exuberant outburst that showers newlyweds with well wishes at the close of the ceremony. Do confirm first with the officiant that it's allowed at the house of worship—some sites object to the clean up required. In recent years, tosses have evolved. Although rice fell out of favor because it was harmful to birds (hence the substitution of birdseed), puffed or hull-less rice is making a comeback. Rose and peony petals are beautifully hued—and biodegradable. Bright streamers and confetti come in endless colors and shapes representing holidays and hobbies, but they are difficult to sweep up and so are best kept indoors. Tosses can be tailored to the season. If pink

No rice or seeds to throw
A substitute we have you know,
Ring this bell loud and clear,
When you see the newlyweds appear,
Its joyful sound will surely convey,
Your love and good wishes on our
"Special Day"
At the reception, again ring the bell,
We'll share a kiss of love, for you as well

Terri and Alex
December 18, 1999

BUBBLE BASKET by Kesley Anderson/My Scrapbook Store. Paper: DMD Industries. Stickers: PrintWorks. Other: bubbles, tulle circles. Fun idea to note: Kesley composed the poem that accompanies these bubble packets.

JINGLE BELL by Lanae Johnson. Fun idea to note: You could create the lettering on a computer, then print as many cards as you need. Hot glue the ribbon and bell to the card.

RICE CONE by Cathy Arnold. Pens: Zig, EK Success. Other: ribbons, silk roses, beads, tulle. Fun idea to note: Cathy wrapped tulle around the paper cone and attached a silk rose and silver beads with ribbon. Inside, she placed puffed rice cereal (instead of rice).

petals are characteristic of spring, then sunflower seeds symbolize summer. In autumn, stuff grass-paper purses with pressed foliage, and capture winter's pristine glaze with punched paper snowflakes cupped in glassine pouches.

Crisp paper cones printed with names and the date become treasured mementos. Experiment with textured paper, deckled edges, and lace doilies, then close the wrap with a monogrammed sticker. (Staples make the strongest seal.) Swathed in tulle, with ribbons and bead ornaments, the cone resembles an ethereal pouf of cloud that has come down to earth (right).

Bubbles, live butterflies, and jingle bells eliminate the issue of litter altogether (just remember that soapy floating orbs can stain satin gowns). Decorate plain plastic bubble bottles with stickers and tulle, then pen a witty poem instructing guests to take a deep breath and blow on their wands (opposite). Or design a card that incorporates a beribboned jingle bell, and suggest that everybody give theirs a joyful good shake (above). 🐚

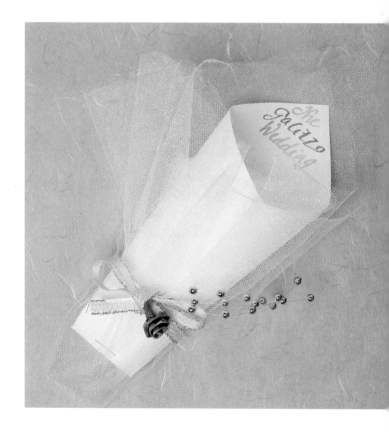

Wedding Albums

WHETHER YOU'RE making your own wedding album or putting together gift scrapbooks for wedding party members, white leather albums are no longer the only option. Colorful cloth and textured papers are available, and trim sizes can range from the traditional upright shape to a horizontal storybook or an accordion-fold booklet.

Binding and Binders

Albums with permanent bindings may have pages that are glued, sewn, or stapled into place. Tied-binding albums, which have stitching on the outside of the spine in the style of traditional Chinese and Japanese books, are a type of permanent album that feels espe-

cially festive. You can buy a hand-made tied-binding album in paper stores and simply personalize the book with your photos and journaling—wedding candids or honeymoon photos are good choices for this type of book. Alternately, you can make your own tied-binding album from a kit, selecting paper, fabric, and ribbon to match the theme and colors of your wedding.

The look of these handmade albums can be exquisite, although the books will be somewhat fragile and unforgiving of mistakes. Thus these and other permanent-bound albums, such as small stapled albums, are best for projects that are clearly defined (such as photos of everyone attending a bridal shower) or formatted in a simple way (a few

photographic highlights you want to share with parents or members of the bridal party).

Binders used for scrapbooking let you add and remove pages easily, a distinct advantage for wedding album projects that may take a while to complete.

The primary binder styles are three-ring binders and expandable spine albums. When considering the type of album or binder to buy, remember that acid-free papers and tissues, along with non-vinyl plastic sleeves, help protect the most precious memorabilia from the damaging effects of light and dust.

Three-ring binders are made to accommodate pages that are 12 x 12 inches, 8½ x 11 inches, or 5½ x 8½ inches. Look for D-shaped rings, which let pages lie flat when the binder is closed and are preferable to binders with O-shaped rings. Design styles of three-ring binders include traditional white

BLUE PHOTO ALBUM by Kelly Edgerton. Album: Newport by Kolo.

HANDMADE ALBUM provided by Books by Hand. Album: Large Ribbon-Bound Album Basic Kit, Books by Hand. Cloth: Hand-stamped book cloth. Organdy ribbon.

THREE WEDDING ALBUMS. *Left.* Frame-a-Name Photo Album by K & Company. Fun idea to note: The cover of this album will hold six- seven- or eight-letter names. *Center.* D-ring binder, Generations by Hazel. *Right.* Post-bound memory album, Generations by Hazel.

as well as colorful cloth versions. Slip-cased three-ring binders store the contents in darkness, sheltering the photos from light, dust, and other pollutants. Its open end allows the binder to slip out under the pressure of its own weight, although snug slipcases may feature thumb notches.

Expandable spine albums include those with a flex-hinge binding, where pages are held in place by small wire loops, and post-bound albums, where pages or perforated sheet protectors are secured by short metal posts. The most common page size for these albums is 12 x 12 inches, although smaller sizes and alternate dimensions can also be found (such as 8 x 10 inches). White wedding covers are available for both types of expandable spine albums.

Mini-Albums

Mini-albums are treasures for those who receive them. Options range from small stapled albums with just twelve pages to small accordion albums or sturdier post-bound albums using 5½ x 8½ inch sheets and sheet protectors.

When assembling individual scrapbooks for close friends and family, several approaches are possible. One way is to keep it simple: Center photos of similar sizes on each page, and let the pictures do the talking. Put all the journaling in one panel at the beginning or end. A second approach is to tell a story. Edit the photographs so that they narrate a slice of the wedding day: Mix one or two portraits

SLIP-CASED BINDER by Hilary Shirley. Binder with slipcase: Preservation Source. *Scrapbook pages.* Plaid paper: Keeping Memories Alive. Computer font: Scrap Rhapsody, Lettering Delights CD Vol 2. Adhesive: Hermafix, Sailor glue pen.

SIMPLY ELEGANT PHOTO ALBUM by Lanae Johnson. Album: Mini paper album with ribbon by Kolo. Adhesive: Photo Mounts, Creative Memories. Fun idea to note: Lanae chose a photo that works well with the ivory color of the album and the ribbon color. She used a color copier to create various sizes of the photo until she found the right scale for the die-cut window.

AUGUST 20, 1999 ALBUM by Megan McMurdie. Album: Luxury Vineyard by Kolo. Stickers: Mrs. Grossman's. Pen: Zig Calligraphy (cover) and Zig Writer (inside), EK Success. Fun idea to note: Megan made her own column die cut.

with just a few candids, alternate close-ups with group shots, and include a couple of still-lifes to set the mood. (But keep color photos with color, black-and-white with black-and-white.)

For an added personal touch, mount the photos in a small album handmade from a kit, using paper, cloth, and ribbon related to the colors of the wedding.

Labeling and Mounting Photos

Commercially processed rolls of film are machine-printed on resin-coated paper. Fiber-based paper is used for prints that are individually developed by hand. To label resin-coated photographs, use a soft graphite pencil, a fine-line marker, or a permanent, fast-drying pen. The pencil adheres to slippery surfaces, and the fast-drying pen protects stacked photos from the inadvertent transfer of ink from the back of one image to the front of another. For fiber-based prints, only use a graphite pencil, never a pen, to write labels.

To prevent an impression from forming on the front, place the photo face down on a hard surface. Never label photos in a stack. Instead, pull them out and mark them one at a time. Write in full names, places, dates, and any other pertinent information, but, as added insurance against making an impression across any faces, try to contain your notes to the edges of the print.

When dropping off wedding snapshots for standard automatic processing, ask if it's possible to have each photo stamped on the back with the number of the roll and the negative number. This will make it easier to order duplicates of great images.

Photos can be mounted several ways. The choice should be based on the value of the images and the purpose of the album. Original prints in a keepsake volume are best protected by photo corners. Glues may be fine for fun mini-scrapbooks featuring duplicate prints.

Corners and slits are two easily reversible methods of photo-mounting. Slits are simply small diagonal cuts in the paper into which the photo's corners are tucked. Use a utility knife to slice these openings, or try one of the special-edged punches sold at craft stores. Corners are available in safe plastics or acid-free papers, in every color from crystal clear to metallic gold to flat black. Glues should only be applied to resin-coated photos: Porous fiber-based prints will absorb the glue. Archival photo mounts offer a dry, safe alternative.

In permanent-bound albums where pages are sewn or stapled together and photos are unprotected, buffer prints by interleaving pages with sheets of unbuffered acid-free tissue. Scrapbooks using plastic sheet protectors will help preserve photos and other page decorations (just be sure to avoid vinyl and acetate sheaths, which are damaging to paper).

Guest Book Variations

Guest books once fulfilled an official function, recording all in attendance at a wedding ceremony. Witnesses would simply sign their name. Today, the albums serve a more sentimental purpose. Family

JAPANESE BINDING ALBUM by Jaime Echt/Crafter's Workshop. Album: Rag & Bone Bindery. Pen: gold gell. Adhesive: double-sided tape. Fun idea to note: Jaime made this bridal shower album for her sister. She placed cardstock rectangles on the page as place-savers for photos that would be developed after the event; at the shower, she had guests write notes around them.

ALBUM WITH HANDMADE REPLY CARD by Renee Comet. Album: Two Women Boxing. Papermaking kit: Original Tin Can Papermaking Kit by Greg Markim. Pen: Sharpie. Fun idea to note: This album pairs candid photos of wedding guests with memorabilia, here a noteworthy reply card. The bride, Lisa Cherkasky, made the paper for her reply cards and invitations; see page 87.

and friends reflect upon the importance of the union and write down their memories of the bride and groom. These inscriptions are among the most meaningful mementos the couple has of the wedding day, and many couples make guest book variations an interesting activity for the reception.

To personalize ready-made guest books, affix your invitation to the cover and add a personal feature to each page: add your initials and the date, or mount a graphic motif (such as a sticker or rubber-stamp design) related to the wedding theme.

Providing envelopes will encourage guests to write longer, more confidential messages, so consider this as a way to expand upon the guest-book concept. Glue envelopes face down on the pages of an album (two or three per page, depending on size) and ask that guests write little letters and tuck them in, creating a book of notes for the bride and groom. Alternately, stock a side table at the reception with brightly colored cards, corresponding envelopes, and plenty of pens. Post a sign asking guests to jot down ideas, quotes, and jokes. They can seal their notes, then drop them into a handcrafted box. Even

more simply, set out a few advice cards with the table settings, along with a brief note asking guests to offer their advice to the bride and groom *(Winter Wedding Place Setting, page 42)*.

At a large reception, provide a guest book at every table rather than having just a single large one. Use small albums, and inscribe the cover of each with the table number. Pen the name of each guest assigned to the table in the upper left-hand corner of a page, and on the opposite, right-hand page, affix photo corners for Polaroid photographs taken by a roving family photographer assigned to get a shot of everyone. Over the course of the meal, guests can pass the book around and write down their thoughts—along with a humorous caption describing the accompanying candid. The artistically inclined might prefer to doodle with colored pencils. Unruled pages allow more room to roam. All that blank space is irresistible!

Some guests need bit of encouragement to take part in an activity set out as part of the place settings, so the bride and groom could ask for their guests' participation as they visit each table. Have

members of the wedding party help out by letting guests know that the bride and groom are looking forward to everyone's comments!

Scrapbook Organizers

Before binders became the home of scrapbooks, they were used for school work or business purposes—so they're natural organizers! The wedding organizer scrapbook is a great idea, whether you're planning a wedding or just trying to sort through all the precious leftover notes, brochures, and receipts you can't bear to part with.

Whether you're making a wedding organizer for yourself or as a gift, start with an acid-free binder. Work with just two or three paper colors and a small set of related ornaments. Place receipts, notes, fabric samples, and pressed flowers right in the sheet protectors, and affix ones that are smaller than the sheet protector size to cardstock. Add journaling to any cardstock backing. Decorate a few pre-made plastic pocket pages (available in office-supply stores) to store brochures or items you might want to remove and examine at a later date.

Section dividers for wedding scrapbook organizers can include:

Phone list	Bridal Gown
Calendar	Bridesmaid's Dress
Music	Photography
Flowers	Invitation
Ceremony Site	Rings
Caterer	Gift Registry

After you slip all the scraps of paper into their sheet protectors, this organizer will have evolved into its higher state—a scrapbook recording the story of your wedding! ✒

PLANNING BINDER by Joy Macdonnell/ My Scrapbook Store. Album: Photo Frame Scrapbook by Hiller. Paper: DMD Industries; Paper Adventures. Stickers: Me & My BIG Ideas. Pockets: Avery Binder Pockets. Fun idea to note: This scrapbook organizer would make a wonderful gift for a bride-to-be. Joy created divider pages for different sections of this organizer; the sheet protectors behind the dividers hold the related receipts and memorabilia.

Scrapbook Page Ideas

AT LAST, TRUE LOVE has come along. You've met the man of your dreams and plan to pledge your heart to him. It's as if everything in the past has been leading up to this point, and your life is only now beginning. Luckily, for this romantic rebirth, you're old enough to know just how precious each moment is—and you're also a scrapbooker! If the prospect of preserving your wedding memories seems daunting, follow these suggestions for stunning spreads.

Select a Theme

Endless love provides endless themes for scrapbook pages *(below)*. The number of strong photos you have per subject will help determine the number of pages the album demands. Some themes may not merit more than a single-page treatment, but spreads give a scrapbook a cohesive, complete feel, so even if the two pages in a spread treat different subjects, subtly connect them with a common element, such as the same paper color.

our
WEDDING
day

Grandpa & Grandma
Wolfley
Nathan & Brenda
Bennett

My parents' yard
made the perfect setting
for a beautiful reception!
We were able to see so
many dear friends and
family. There were so
many guests that the
receiving line went
from 6:30 to 10:30 pm!
It was a wonderful night!

JUNE 14
1997

The Garden Reception
CLINTON, UTAH

SCOTT
and
STEPH

August 13, 1998
SALT LAKE CITY, UTAH

ENDLESS LOVE by Brenda Bennett. Mulberry paper: Personal Stamp Exchange. Embossed paper: Solum. Pens: Micron Pigma, Sakura; Milky Gel Roller, Pentel. Colored pencils: Prismacolor, Sanford. Photo corners: Canson. Fun idea to note: Brenda embossed the flowers using a light box.

OUR WEDDING DAY by Brenda Bennett. Pens: Micron Pigma, Sakura; Zig Scroll & Brush, EK Success. Colored pencils: Prismacolor, Sanford. Photo frames and corners: K & Co. Fun idea to note: Brenda cut out the flowers and leaves from stationery she had on hand.

SCOTT AND STEPH by Brenda Bennett. Pens: Zig Writer and Zig Scroll & Brush, EK Success. Photo corners: K & Co.

LOVE

makes the world go 'round!

August 13
1 9 9 8

the
Reception

Scott & Stephanie both looked great at their reception! The reception line went like this: Mom & Dad Marilyn & Kelly Badily, Justin Badily, Randy Badily, Jason Badily, T.J. Mitchell, Brice Mitchell, Trent Dalton, Scott & Stephanie, Lori Sorensen, Schawny Manning, Rebecca Waymetti, Jill Badily, Brenda Bennett, & Jenette Mitchell. Lucky for them they were able to escape early and be off to their wedding night destination around 9 pm!

Once again, Mom and Dad's yard provided the perfect setting for a garden reception. The flowers, orchard, and gazebo looked so beautiful. We all had fun taking pictures and greeting all the guests that came to give their regards to the happy new couple.

Choose a Focal Photo

After deciding on a theme—be it for a single-page, several spreads, or an entire scrapbook—sort your photos into categories. This helps to break down a seemingly overwhelming task into manageable steps. Next, if necessary, further narrow your focus to the subject that will be treated on one spread. Out of these images, select those that have strong color, sharp definition, good lighting, and distinct character. Don't feel obligated to use every shot: Weed out the weak photos. Finally, choose a focal photo for the page or spread: It should be the one that best captures the featured event.

Paper Color and Texture

A simple color scheme helps unify an album. Consider using two or three shades from your wedding palette or choose hues that will pick up the colors in your photos (*Staker's* and *McMurdie's*). Experiment by placing your focal shot on top of

LOVE MAKES THE WORLD GO 'ROUND by Brenda Bennett. Pens: Zig Writer and Zig Scroll & Brush, EK Success. Flowers: Nature's Pressed.

THE RECEPTION PAGES by Brenda Bennett. Patterned paper: Paper Patch. Stickers: Mrs. Grossman's. Photo corners stamp: Stampin' Up! Pen: Micron Pigma, Sakura. Colored pencils: Prismacolor, Sanford. Colorless blender: Sanford. Computer font: CK Script, "Best of Creative Lettering" CD Vol 1, *Creating Keepsakes*.

PEEK-A-BOOS AND KISSES by Kelly Edgerton. Album: Newport by Kolo. Patterned paper: Keeping Memories Alive. Vellum: Making Memories. Punches: Family Treasures; All Night Media. Pen: Zig Writer, EK Success. Computer font: CK Concave, "Wedding Alphabet" CD, *Creating Keepsakes*.

AND TWO SHALL BECOME ONE by Kelly Edgerton. Paper: DMD. Punches: McGill; Emagination; All Night Media. Border template: Coluzzle, Provo Craft. Pens: Zig Writer, EK Success. Pencils: Draw & Paint, Stampin'Up! Chalks: Close to My Heart, D.O.T.S. Scissors: Victorian and Scallop by Fiskars. Computer fonts: CK Script, "The Best of Creative Lettering" CD Vol 1, *Creating Keepsakes*; Fancy, *Lettering Delights Deluxe* CD.

WITH THIS RING by Kesley Anderson. Mulberry paper: AccuCut. Banner: Cock-A-Doodle Designs. Die cut: Stampin Station. Corner rounder: Marvy Uchida. Design line: "Larkspur," Mrs. Grossman's. Scissors: Seagull by Fiskars. Pen: Gelly Roll, Sakura. Chalk: Graf-T Products. Lettering: Wedding Journal Genie.

different sample papers and observing how each alters the impact of the image.

Textured or patterned papers give scrapbooks a luxurious, tactile quality, tempting readers to reach out and touch the page. But like beading and lace on a bridal gown, textured paper usually works best as an accent. Note that most handmade papers contain lignin and/or acid, either of which will yellow and wither whatever they come in contact with. The effects can be lessened if such paper is treated with a deacidification spray such as Archival Mist.

Cropping and Matting Photos

Cropping and matting are two different crafts that share the same objective: to spotlight part of a photo. A cropped photo is trimmed, either into a smaller standard format (the oval portraits *In Love Makes the*

With This Ring...

Tim Betsy

Mr. and Mrs. Nyman

Naperville Illinois Summer, 98

Tim & Betsy
a beautiful
couple. The ceremony
was a short service
performed by Father
Doug.

Father Doug was the
priest at Tim & Betsy's
college. Tim & Betsy
smiled at each other
through the ceremony.

Mr. and Mrs. Nyman

World Go 'Round) or a silhouette (the bended knee of *Peek-A-Boos and Kisses*). Crop to cut out any superfluous, distracting details, but be careful not to carve off anything that might, a couple of decades down the road, add to the value of the image. A matted photo is "framed" by one or more paper borders in order to emphasize its importance.

Creative Titles

The title of a spread should claim a dominant spot on the page to anchor the photos and it should clearly indicate the subject, but that doesn't mean it has to be literal. A marriage is a joyous event—it's okay to have some fun with words, especially if the topic is lighthearted. Why just call a page "My Engagement Ring" when it could be the cheekier "Diamonds are a Girl's Best Friend"?

If hand-drawing your title, common sense suggests that practice makes perfect. In fact, to avoid the risks altogether, draft titles on smaller, separate pieces of paper. If you make a mistake, toss the trial run and start over. Frame the finished title with a mat.

Whether you draw it by hand or print it out on your PC, tailor the color and style of your lettering to the page's photos. Just be sure to use a powder-based toner if taking the computer route; because the ink in liquid inkjet cartridges is water-soluble, print will run if exposed to moisture and will discolor over time.

Title pages—those that decorate the front or inside cover of a single-subject volume (or begin a new section within a large, multi-subject scrapbook)—merit special attention. Rather than clutter

WEDDING MEMORIES by Jenny Jackson. Paper: The Natural Paper Co. Stamp: D.O.T.S. Computer fonts: CK Script, "Creating Keepsakes Lettering" CD Vol 1, *Creating Keepsakes;* CK Crooked Classic, "Creating Keepsakes Wedding Lettering" CD, *Creating Keepsakes.* Ribbon: Offray. Deckling ruler. Fun idea to note: For this title page, Jenny used a deckling ruler to give a hand-torn look to the two strips of paper by the spine of the album.

OUR FAMILY TREE by Jenny Jackson. Paper: The Natural Paper Co. Computer fonts: CK Script, "Creating Keepsakes Lettering" CD Vol 1, *Creating Keepsakes;* CK Leafy Capitals, "Creating Keepsakes Wedding Lettering" CD, *Creating Keepsakes.* Ribbon: Offray. Fun idea to note: Jenny created this page to be the title page for a homemade wedding album.

HERE COMES THE BRIDE by Jenny Jackson. Paper: Keeping Memories Alive. Punch: Family Treasures. Computer fonts: CK Cursive and CK Journaling, "Creating Keepsakes Lettering" CD Vol 2, *Creating Keepsakes;* CK Crooked Classic, "Creating Keepsakes Wedding Lettering" CD, *Creating Keepsakes.* Fun idea to note: Instead of just writing down the date and place, Jenny journaled a hysterical anecdote — about buying her wedding dress — directly onto the check-patterned paper.

OH BEAUTIFUL DAY by Brenda Bennett. Patterned paper: Colors By Design. Mulberry paper: Personal Stamp Exchange. Spiral punch: Marvy Uchida. Pen: Milky Gel Roller, Pentel. Colored pencils: Prismacolor, Sanford. Fun idea to note: Simple geometric shapes are pleasing to the eye: Brenda cropped to literally "circle in" on the close-up of her and her husband, then counterbalanced this image with the rectangular shot, which reveals important background details.

them with copious photos and long captions, stick to a powerful single image and a straightforward title. *Wedding Memories* incorporates many handsome papers, but the title itself is short and sweet.

Journaling

Speaking of stories, photos can't do all the talking. Journaling explains the who, what, when, where, and why of a spread. Start with the facts: If not on the individual spreads, then at least in one place in the album, jot down the names (first and last) of everyone on display, the place, and the dates—including the year (by 2032, 1997 will seem . . . well, a century ago). Next, write out the anecdotes that had guests laughing (or sobbing, or struck silent). And get your husband in on the journaling—he was there, too!

Script out a rough draft of your text before inking it: It will give you a chance to edit the story,

AUGUST 20, 1999 by Megan McMurdie.
Patterned paper: Colors By Design. Pen: Zig
Writer, EK Success.

HAPPILY EVER AFTER by Megan McMurdie.
Patterned paper: Penny Black. Pen: Zig
Calligraphy and Zig Writer, EK Success.

A FAIRY TALE WEDDING by Cathy Arnold.
Yellow diamond dust paper: Paper Adventures.
Stickers and design line: Mrs. Grossman's.
Fun idea to note: Cathy cut out the *Snow
White* scene from a shower invitation!

FROM PAPER DOLLS TO A PRINCESS by
Cathy Arnold. Patterned paper: Paper Patch.
Stickers: Making Memories. Design line:
Mrs. Grossman's. Corners: 3L. Fun idea to
note: The paper doll's dress and veil exactly
matched the bride's dress and veil!

check your spelling, and gauge how much space the journaling will require. Like titles, journaling can be matted on borders and treated as pieces of art.

Arrange and Adhere

Before gluing anything down, try out different configurations of your photos, titles, and journaling. Go for balance: Ideally, the eye should move easily from one point to another. As a general guideline, the layout of elements on a spread often follows the up-and-down of a "W" (*And Two Shall Become One*); on a single page, the zig-zag of a "Z" (*Oh Beautiful Day*).

When you're pleased with the arrangement, secure all the elements to the page using a safe adhesive: Check the label to confirm the product is acrylic-based. It's still preferable to mount the most precious photos and original documents, such as certificates or invitations, with acid-free paper or plastic corners (*...to a Princess*). They're available in a range of colors and allow for easy removal of the mounted artwork.

Experiment with Extras . . .

. . . but keep it simple. Stickers, rubber stamps, die cuts and punches, dried flowers, ribbons, and other ephemera can personalize a page, but be careful of cluttering spreads with too much of a good thing. Simplicity connotes elegance and class, which is appropriate for a wedding album. Let the motto "Less is more" inspire you. Save clusters of tiny stickers for other projects, and focus on a few striking ornaments, such as the solitary, felt-trimmed, long-stemmed rose on *The Reception (opposite, bottom)*, or the three hand-embossed blossoms that pick up the pattern of the background paper on *Endless Love*. Fabric trimmed from a seam of your gown or

A DAY TO REMEMBER by Heather Thatcher. Patterned paper: Printworks. Vellum: Sonborn. Laser cut: Paper Lace. Pens: Zig Millenium, EK Success. Pencils: Berol Prismacolor.

THE RECEPTION by Heather Thatcher. Patterned paper: Printworks (red with gold); Paper Adventures (behind rose velvet). Vellum: Frances Meyer. Laser cut: Paper Lace. Pens: Zig Writer, EK Success. Pencils: Berol Prismacolor.

STAKER'S by Megan McMurdie. Patterned paper: Woobie Prints. Pen: Zig Calligraphy and Zig Writer, EK Success.

MCMURDIE'S by Megan McMurdie. Patterned paper: Lasting Impressions for Paper. Pen: Zig Calligraphy and Zig Writer, EK Success.

Lance & Brandy Edwards
April 26, 1994

Kris and I started our road trip off by driving to Logan, Utah for our roommate Brandy's wedding. It was so exciting to see our roommate in her wedding gown coming out of the Logan Temple with Lance. Brandy looked beautiful.

This picture makes me & Kris gag because Brandy looks like such a twig between us! Having 3 engaged roommates this semester definitely made life interesting! It was actually a lot of fun looking at dresses & engagement pictures with them & being part of all the excitement & pre-wedding jitters!

LANCE AND BRANDY by Hilary Shirley. Patterned paper: Keeping Memories Alive (plaid). Computer fonts: Scrap Rhapsody, *Lettering Delights* CD Vol. 2. Adhesive: Hermafix; Sailor glue pen.

MEMORY GROVE by Heather Thatcher. Patterned paper: Frances Meyer (tan with dots). Laser cut: Paper Lace. Pens: Zig Writer, EK Success. Pencils: Berol Prismacolor. Chalks: Koss. Fun idea to note: Heather designed her own columns for this page.

BEAUTIFUL BRIDE-TO-BE by Heather Thatcher. Vellum: Paper Company. Punches: Family Treasures; Circles punch: McGill. Pens: Zig Writer, EK Success. Pencils: Berol Prismacolor.

left over after a fitting, instructions from the caterer, and airport boarding passes are the kinds of details that will make your scrapbook unique; if you're concerned about the acid content of such items, place them in memorabilia pockets or neutralize them with a spray. Rubber stamps can be used for decorative borders, but to protect neighboring photos from potentially harmful chemicals in stamping ink, seal the stamped impressions with a clear embossing powder—like a clear top coat of nail polish, it will also help the color of the stamp last longer. Computer clip art and color photocopies can add incredibly realistic-looking graphics to your scrapbook. Print or photocopy on acid- and lignin-free paper (today, many regular office papers are acid-free), and use a printer or photocopier that works with a powder toner, which is permanent. ✍

Creative Lettering

THE WEDDING INVITATION has been proofread and printed, each carefully considered word suitably centered, swathed in tissues or veils of vellum, tucked into the traditional two envelopes and sent on its way. Now it's time to take a break from all that formality and bring out the colored markers. Creative lettering can ornament all sorts of things: bridal shower and bachelor party invitations (the three alphabets here may not be quite right for the guys, but use your imagination); signs at the reception marking, for example, the coat check, the favor table, or the powder room; the "Just Married!" poster on your getaway car; scrapbook pages; and thank-you notes.

Before embarking on a bout of creative lettering, keep the following recommendations in mind. Number one, start with a number two. *Pencil*, that is. There's a reason—it has an eraser. Lightly sketch out the framework of the word or phrase first, add on decorative elements, trace in ink, then get the

lead out by gently erasing any leftover pencil marks. Once you've outlined your title, consider making regular black-and-white photocopies. These allow you to experiment with different color combinations before finalizing the "master." And because the graphic letters command a lot of attention, reserve them for key words, and keep conjunctions and such in small, inconspicuous cursive *(above)*.

Wedding Rose

Promise a rose garden with this pretty floral font, perfect for table numbers and other signs at an outdoor, springtime brunch. To draw block letters (ignore the blooms for a moment), begin by penciling the single-line skeleton of the word or phrase, making sure to leave enough space between letters

FOR THE BRIDE AND GROOM SIGN by Heather Thatcher. Green paper: Paper Adventures. Pens: Zig, EK Success. Colored pencils: Berol Prismacolor.

WEDDING ROSE ALPHABET by Heather Thatcher. Pens: Zig, EK Success. Colored pencils: Berol Prismacolor.

for the final block shape. Using a ruler if necessary, draw a parallel line on either side of the central skeletal line to build the block, and add the squat square ends, or serifs, as indicated in the sample alphabet. Curve a line up the letter, then double it, for the vine. To create the rose blossom, draw a loose, imperfect circle, and add a swirl in the center for petals. Ink only the outline of the letter and the climbing rose ornament, and after it dries, erase any remaining sketch marks. Then color to your heart's content.

Wedding Column

Delicate swirly serifs dress the classical columns of this stately alphabet, and its gradational color makes it a particularly expert match with marbled paper *(above right)*. The columns also pick up the vertical lines in pinstriped stationery *(above left)*. Refer to the sample, and spell out the word or phrase in pencil, being sure to allow enough room between the letters for the columns. Then draw the columns out of blocks and squared serifs. (Use a ruler if your hand is unsteady.) Note that the column essentially looks like a fat capital letter "I". Often, as in "A" or "K",

the column is part of the standard structure of the letter, but in round letters such as "C", the column simply decorates the center of the shape.

Wedding Block

Small buds embellish the streamlined block letters of this alphabet, but they can be replaced with any other cute motif: a bowtie, for example, or butterfly.

PLEASE LEAVE CAMERAS HERE SIGN by Heather Thatcher. Patterned paper: Ever After (green stripe); marbled cardstock. Pens: Zig, EK Success. Colored pencils: Berol Prismacolor.

COAT CHECK SIGN by Heather Thatcher. Pens: Zig, EK Success. Colored pencils: Berol Prismacolor.

WEDDING COLUMN ALPHABET by Heather Thatcher. Pens: Zig, EK Success. Colored pencils: Berol Prismacolor.

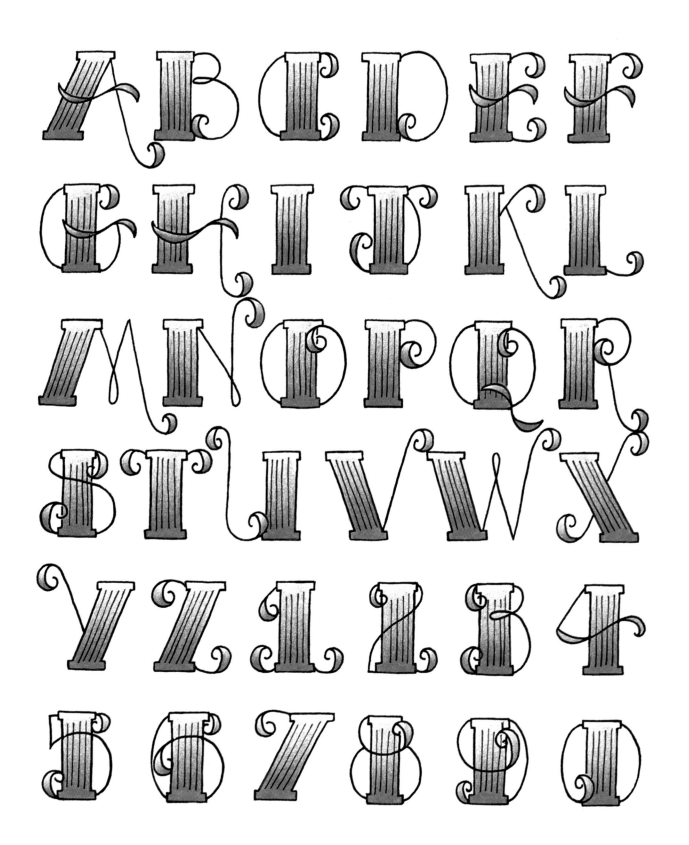

Customize the art according to your wedding theme. The paper mats for the just married sign *(below)* complement both the color and the pattern of the lettering—note the embossed buds on the white border. To create the gradational color effect shown in guest book *(below)*, use colored pencils—three from the same family, dark, medium, and light. Start with the darkest color at the top of the letter and gently shade about a third. Then switch to the medium hue, overlapping the edges of the darkest pencil so that it's difficult to see where one color ends and the next begins. Repeat with the palest shade for the bottom third of the block.

For more lettering ideas, refer to *The Art of Creative Lettering*, by Becky Higgins *(see Resources).*

JUST MARRIED SIGN by Heather Thatcher. Patterned paper: Lasting Impressions (embossed); Printworks (purple dot); O'Scrap (purple check). Pens: Zig, EK Success. Colored pencils: Berol Prismacolor.

GUEST BOOK SIGN by Heather Thatcher. Pink vine paper: Colors by Design. Pens: Zig, EK Success. Colored pencils: Berol Prismacolor.

WEDDING BLOCK ALPHABET by Heather Thatcher. Pens: Zig, EK Success. Colored pencils: Berol Prismacolor.

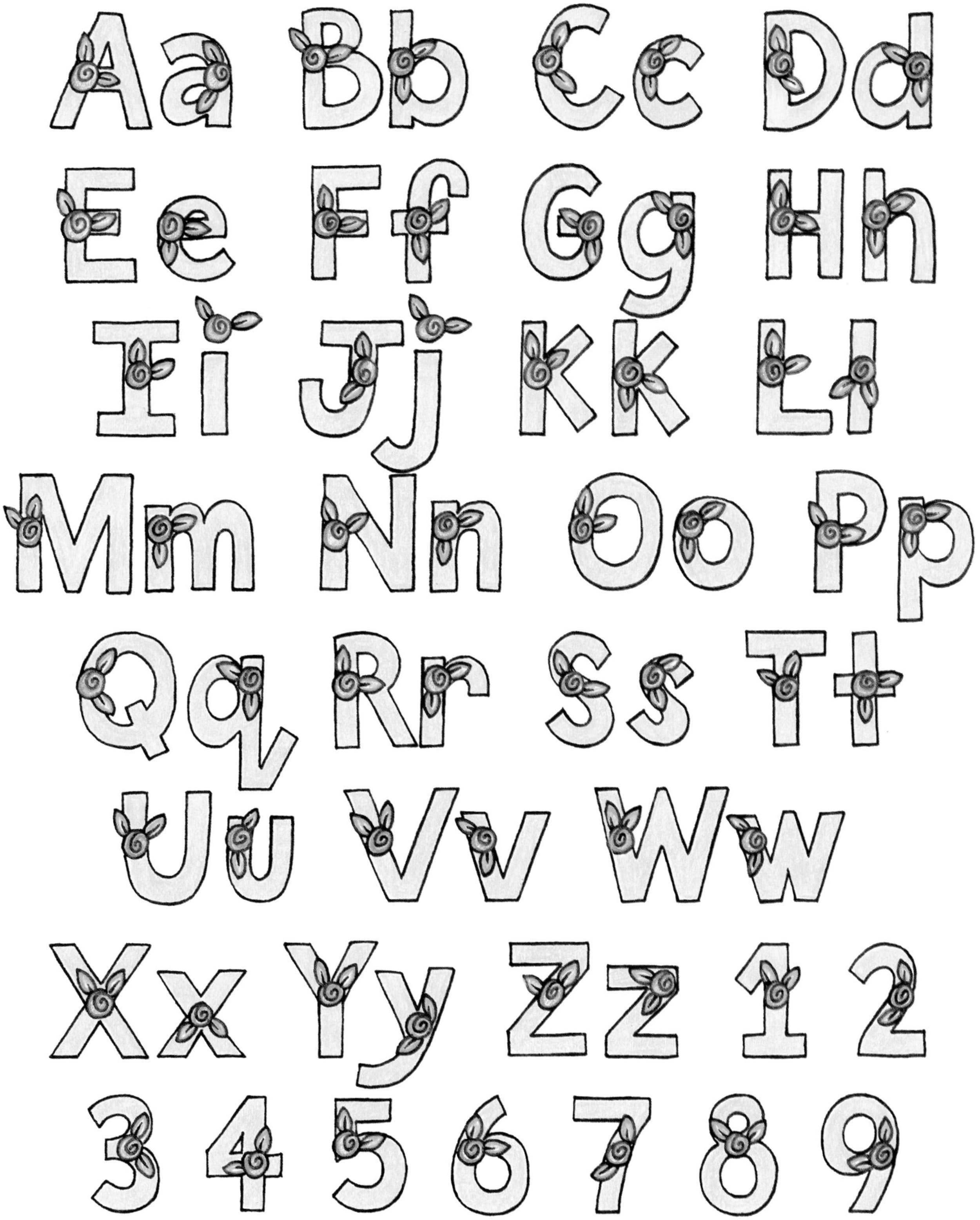

Aa Bb Cc Dd
Ee Ff Gg Hh
Ii Jj Kk Ll
Mm Nn Oo Pp
Qq Rr Ss Tt
Uu Vv Ww
Xx Yy Zz 1 2
3 4 5 6 7 8 9

Frames & Displays

THE PORTRAITS will be framed. That goes without saying. The classic black-and-white of you and your beau belongs on the mantelpiece in your den or wall in your bedroom. But don't overlook other bits of memorabilia. The invitation *(below)*, handwritten vows and toasts, quaint proverbs and romantic poems, the exotic stamp on the postcard you sent to yourselves from your honeymoon abroad, bouquet flowers, bridal lace, or an exquisitely colored leaf that encapsulates the season: All these items make beautiful, personal decorations.

Framed images can also enhance the wedding itself *(see Photography)*. Whimsical signs, colorfully matted or placed in inexpensive store-bought frames *(see Creative Lettering)*, can welcome guests to the site, direct them to powder rooms, and remind them to turn off their cell phones during the ceremony. Hand-decorated frames, wrapped in petal paper or trimmed with dried flowers, make wonderful favors. Very small frames used as place cards can be taken home at the end of the evening, and guests can eventually substitute the nameplate with a commemorative photo. A mixed collection of small-to-medium sized frames from rummage sales and discount stores dresses up table numbers at a funky semiformal wedding.

Framing Certificates

Before framing your wedding certificate *(opposite right)*, it's smart to deacidify it. Papers are often made from commercial materials and wood pulp, and these contain acid and lignin, both of which increase the rate of yellowing, fading, and deterioration. The safest way to deacidify a certificate is to spray it with a product specifically made for this purpose. The spray neutralizes the acid content of the paper without causing the potentially non-waterproof ink of the signatures to run. To deacidify, lay the certificate face down on tissue paper, shake the spray bottle well, and mist the back side of the

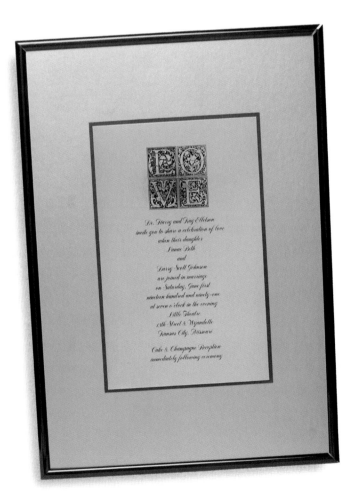

paper first. Apply a light, even coating, keeping the nozzle about six inches from the paper's surface. Then repeat on the front side of the certificate, and let it dry thoroughly.

To account for the expansion and contraction of a paper or photograph in response to changes in temperature and humidity, the dimensions of the frame should always be slightly larger than those of the print. If a frame is fitted too tightly, it may cause the certificate to pucker when it expands. Frames that use spring clips to hold the backing board in place permit greater flexibility than those with a more rigid system of paper wedges.

When mounting certificates, avoid the use of tape or glue: Even safe glue can travel through the back of porous papers and destroy the embellished front. The best adhesives are reversible. Mounting corners, which eliminate the risk of the certificate ripping if you ever decide to remove it from its

FRAMED LOVE WEDDING INVITATION provided by Lanae Johnson. Fun idea to note: This frame, which was given to Lanae as a wedding gift, coordinates with her invitation.

HANDMADE PAPER DISPLAY by Lisa Cherkasky. Papermaking kit: Original Tin Can Kit by Greg Markim. Pen: Sharpie. Fun idea to note: Lisa made the paper from movie stubs, theater programs, and other memorabilia she collected during her engagement.

WEDDING CERTIFICATE by Hilary Shirley. Frame: National Picture and Frame Company. Patterned paper: Frances Meyer. Vellum: Sonburn. Fun idea to note: Hilary scanned the certificate into her computer and then printed it onto vellum. She placed the vellum over patterned paper to achieve this special effect.

frame, are available in colored acid-free papers and safe plastics such as Mylar and polypropylene.

Framing Photos

Never crop one-of-a-kind photos. Crafters sometimes get "crop crazy," cutting photos to fit the creative demands of their pages. But if an image is important enough to frame, consider what you're cropping out before you pick up those scissors. Cropping is meant to emphasize the most significant elements in a photo. If you're inadvertently trimming off telling details—scenic clues which indicate the time, place, or people involved—you'll damage the integrity of the image and excise some future memories in the process. Make duplicates, and experiment on those instead.

A creative alternative to cropping is matting.

A mat acts as a buffer, preventing a photograph's emulsion from sticking to the glass cover. It also acts as a border, framing a photo within the frame, showcasing certain elements of the image without actually, physically, permanently cutting off others. The geometrical shape of the mat can mirror that of the outer frame—big rectangle, little rectangle—or can contrast with it—a circle within a square.

Individual prints (as opposed to regularly processed roles of film) are usually made with a border that should not be trimmed, because it indicates the smallest size the accompanying frame ought to be. As an extension of this border, the mat should complement the photo in shade and size. The color of the mat affects the color of the print. For example, a pink mat will pick up the pinks in a bridal bouquet, while a busy decorative motif might

detract from the image and reduce its impact. Be careful of overly large mats: Although the look is in vogue, and can beautifully spotlight a small photo, it can also overpower it. The photo should not take second place to its frame.

Craft stores sell pre-cut mats in a variety of shapes, colors, and sizes, but if you want to trim your own, first decide on the geometrical shape of your frame within a frame. Then find the center of your board and, using a ruler or stencil, lightly outline the shape in pencil on the *front* of it. Cutting out from the front gives a cleaner edge, because paper fibers are being pushed toward the back. If fibers are still visible after cutting, use a clean nail file to smooth. Gently erase any remaining pencil marks.

If you've cut out a frame that leaves space for the backboard to show through *(Handmade Paper Display, page 87)*, attach the photo to the front of the backboard using a safe adhesive and make sure to glue down the corners, which have a tendency to curl over time. If the mat will completely conceal the edges of the photo, so that no backboard shows through *(On Your Special Day, page 91)*, attach the photo to the back of the mat.

More than one mat can be layered within a frame to create a beveled look. For example, a maroon-colored mat with a proportionately smaller circle sits beneath the top, silver-gray mat of the *Handmade Paper Display*. In addition, special cutters, also available at craft stores, allow you to bevel individual boards, so that both the front, surface color of the mat and the paler shade of the undyed board beneath frame the photo. (For information on mounting photos, see *Memory Books*.)

Safe Framing

Many attractive frame styles—in wood or metal, carved, stained, painted, or gilded—are available for

A TIME TO REMEMBER by Kelly Edgerton. Mat: "Frame a Name" by K & Co. Paper: D.O.T.S. cream parchment. Computer font: CK Calligraphy, "The Best of Creative Lettering" CD Vol I, *Creating Keepsakes*. Fun idea to note: A lovely gift for a flower girl!

HANDMADE PAPER FRAME by Diane Hackley. Frame kit: Books By Hand. Handmade paper: Black Inc. Handmade silk paper: Hero Arts. Scissors: Fiskars. Adhesive: Yes glue. Paper flowers by Modern Romance. Fun idea to note: Diane tied the two paper flowers to her frame with the ribbon; you could put the flowers on the top, or on the bottom, of the frame – whichever works best with the photo you will be putting inside.

DOUBLE PAPER FRAME provided by Books by Hand. Frame kit: Books by Hand, #K117.

purchase, and many pretty papers can be used to wrap thin, plain plywood frames but not all of these are of archival quality. If you're concerned about preserving framed papers and photos, use duplicates whenever possible, and choose safe materials.

Certain household adhesives, such as rubber cement, which is petroleum-based, damage photos and paper. A safe adhesive is: acrylic- or starch-based; solid (liquids absorb into paper, causing it to pucker); non-toxic; acid-free; reversible; odorless when wet; and colorless when dry. Glue sticks are good, as are acid-free photo mounts and safe tape. The less used, the better.

FLORAL PRINT FRAMES by Lanae Johnson. Frames: Dioni. Mats: Picture This Victorian Collection by Mastermount (Riley Mountain Products). Adhesive: photo mounts, Creative Memories. Fun idea to note: Lanae color copied the photos, adjusting the colors to create an older, warmer feel.

Glass helps to protect paper from dirt and filter out ultraviolet light. Picture glass is clear; non-reflective glass has a slightly mottled surface that prevents reflections; and Uf3 filtered glass filters out 85 to 95 percent of the light that fades photographs.

Mats tend to be acidic, so be sure to look for high-grade, acid-free boards. Wood frames also contain acid, which will eventually migrate to both photos and paper, unless they have had a sealer, such as urethane or shellac, applied to the inside edge. Or, you can apply a clear acrylic finish to the back of the frame yourself. The card- or corrugated board packed with store-bought frames has a high acid content. Cut your own backing from acid-free core-board. Paper backing, used to keep dust out, is acidic, too, and should be substituted with an acid-free, lignin-free sheet. ✍

WEDDING ANNOUNCEMENT by Hilary Shirley. Frame: Intercraft. Transparency paper: Great White. Hilary scanned the photo, adjusting the size; she used her software to feather the edges of the photo. She then printed the photo onto transparency paper and trimmed it to overlay the announcement.

ROSE FRAME by Susana Espinosa. Frame: gold frame, oval photo mat. Rubber stamps: Romantic Rose, Romantic Rose Large Bouquet, and "On Your Special Day" by Rubber Stampede. Pens/Pencils: gold marker; watercolor pencils. Other: inkpad by Rubber Stampede; gold powder, burgundy cardstock.

Keepsake Boxes

IN ALL THE HAPPY chaos of planning a wedding and reception, it's easy to lose sight of the sweet ever after. But in order to preserve the precious mementos of your most perfect union, so that generations to come can cherish them, too, it's essential to take a few precautions. With the proper care, your bouquet can decorate your bedroom for years, your invitation will look as crisp as the day it was printed—and your daughter just might walk down the aisle wearing your wedding dress.

Storage Boxes

Once upon a time, mothers spent months on end stitching table linens and monogramming sheets in preparation for their daughter's marriage. As soon as a girl got engaged, this bridal trousseau was stocked even more, with lingerie, pots and pans, anything she could use to set up her new home. The modern-day hope chest reflects this charming custom. But when it comes to safeguarding ephemera from the effects of time, wooden boxes won't do. Dresser

drawers, plastic trunks, and shoe boxes all contain harmful agents that will eventually migrate to papers, photos, and fabrics, resulting in yellowing, fading, and overall deterioration. The best way to protect materials is to store them in acid- and lignin-free cardboard boxes that cannot be sealed *(Three Archival Boxes, page 96)*. These boxes shield items from light and pollutants while still allowing enough breathing room to prevent condensation or mildew from forming. Because conservation is a common concern today, such archival boxes are available in many sizes.

You don't have to wait until after the wedding, however, to put keepsake boxes to use. Decorate one in the colors of your palette, and cut a small mail slot out of the top. Place it on the favors table at the reception site alongside a stack of blank cards and envelopes, and ask guests to drop you a note from the party. You and your husband can enjoy these little letters upon returning from your honeymoon. Or decorate a lidded box with favorite quotes and festive ornaments and set it out as a mailbox for wedding cards *(United in Marriage, page 94)*.

BRIDAL KEEPSAKES by Kelly Edgerton. Box: Bridal Keepsake Case (open and closed) by Highsmith. Scissors: 12" rotary trimmer with deckle blade by Fiskars. Punches: Family Treasures. Stickers: Me & My BIG Ideas. Computer fonts: CK Script, "Best of Creative Lettering" CD Vol 1, *Creating Keepsakes;* CK Flair, "Wedding Alphabet" CD, *Creating Keepsakes.* Adhesive: 3L photo tape. Ribbon: Offray.

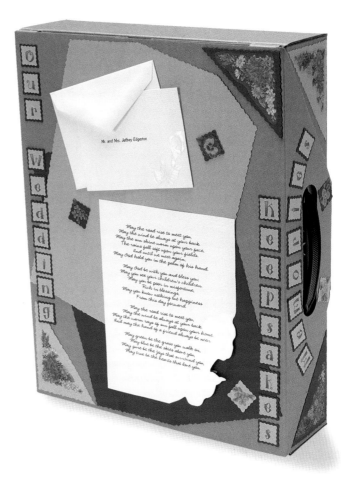

Preserving Paper

Doctors advise that "an ounce of prevention is worth a pound of cure," and this aphorism also holds true for the health of your papers. The key to keeping your wedding stationery in tip-top shape is to start with the right type of paper. Print on acid-free, lignin-free stock, and you're at least halfway there.

Paper produced from wood pulp contains lignin, a natural component that binds fibers together. Over time, lignin causes yellowing when it comes in contact with light and humidity, and acid—used during the paper-making process to break down wood fibers—causes the paper to become brittle and brown. Both chemicals result in yellowing, discoloration, and deterioration.

Two types of acid- and lignin-free paper are commercially available: Buffered brands are manufactured with calcium carbonate, an element that neutralizes acid and stabilizes pH; unbuffered brands are not. In general, buffered brands offer added insurance, but they do increase the rate at which a photo's emulsion deteriorates, so it's better to go with unbuffered when the paper will come in contact with photographs.

If you've read the label and you're still not sure, you can check a paper's pH with either a special pen, for white to ivory stock, or a testing strip, for darker colored sheets. Both are available at archival supply stores. The pen test is a piece of cake: Simply scribble a few words—"Just Married!"—on the paper in question. Chlorophenol red, a chemical in the ink, will respond by either turning yellow or purple. Yellow equals acidic; purple, alkaline. The pH strip requires a bit more effort, and involves dampening a section of a sample page with distilled water. Carefully follow the instructions on the package.

Even acid- and lignin-free paper is susceptible to the elements. High temperatures increase the rate of aging, while drastic shifts in temperature cause paper to expand and contract, stretching out fibers. The ideal climate? Sixty-five to 68 degrees Fahrenheit. Humidity also undermines the integrity of paper. Too much moisture in the air encourages the growth of mold, fades inks, and discolors papers, while too little can leave sheets brittle. Insects and rodents feast on papers, so be sure to protect documents in archival boxes. Both fluorescent and ultraviolet lights discolor. And air-born pollutants, from cleaning fumes and aerosols, attack even the hardiest stock.

Newspaper contains a whole lot of lignin—just think how the newspaper yellows when left out on the porch too long. But you can preserve your published engagement and wedding announcements. First, make copies on acid- and lignin-free stock (be sure to use a machine that prints with powder toner, which is permanent). Next, deacidify the original. The sooner you do it, the newer the newspaper, the less likely it is to yellow. To do this, immerse the clipping in a shallow glass casserole dish or stainless steel baking pan filled with distilled water, let soak for about 20 minutes, then carefully remove and leave to dry on a clean, flat surface. And don't be afraid of the water: Rinsing removes acidic dust, and the wet fibers expand and bond, making the newspaper stronger.

Archival Mist can also be employed to deacidify newspaper, as well as handmade papers, letters, and marriage certificates, all of which may feature handwriting in inks that would run if washed. This spray is non-toxic, non-flammable, and odor-free and will not alter inks, adhesives, or dyes.

UNITED IN MARRIAGE by Kelly Edgerton. Wedding card box: Highsmith. Mulberry paper: PrintWorks. Circle set, birch, and small swirl punches: Family Treasures. Grapevine leaf punch: Emagination. Swirl border punch: All Night Media. Stickers: "Verdigris Vines" Paper Whispers, Mrs. Grossman's. Computer fonts: CK Leafy Capitals, "Wedding Alphabet" CD, *Creating Keepsakes;* CK Calligraphy, "The Best of Creative Lettering" CD Vol 1, *Creating Keepsakes.* Adhesives: Xyron Machine; Scotch Document Mending Tape. Fun idea to note: Kelly carefully lined the inside of the cut-out card slot with heavy tape to keep it from fraying.

One final word of advice: Acid migrates and will contaminate other paper items (even those that are acid-free) if they are stored together. So make sure acidic and acid-free items are stored separately.

Preserving Flowers

Before you toss your bouquet to a gaggle of clamoring girlfriends, consider this: Dried flowers can be used to decorate mirror and picture frames, can be pressed on the pages of a special floral journal, and, of course, can be arranged in a vase as a table centerpiece. More and more brides are ordering two bouquets—one to throw, and one to take home. In fact, if you inform your florist in advance that you'll be ordering a second bouquet after you return from your honeymoon, the flowers will be in that much better condition for drying since preservation works best when flowers are fresh but free of moisture, which can cause spotting. If you do decide to dry

THREE ARCHIVAL BOXES. Microfiche Box (top) by Metal Edge. This box is perfect for storing corsages, gloves, and memorabilia. 8 x 10" Box (middle) by Metal Edge. This keepsake box could store a table centerpiece, shoes, or photos. 10 x 12" Box (bottom) by University Products. This flat box is large enough to store a hat, short veil, or paper memorabilia. Fun idea to note: These acid- and lignin-free boxes do not seal shut; air is not trapped with the items inside, which helps preserve your keepsakes. (Photo by Al Thelin.)

OUR WEDDING DAY KEEPSAKES by Kelly Edgerton. Storage box: Highsmith. Computer font: CK Flair, "Wedding Alphabet" CD, Creating Keepsakes. Pens: Zig Writer, EK Success. Pencils: Memory Pencils, EK Success. Chalks: Close to My Heart, D.O.T.S. Adhesive: 3L photo tape. Raffia curling straw.

your original bouquet, or your fiancé's boutonnière, or a centerpiece from the reception, ask your maid of honor, your mom, or another friend to store these in the freezer until you get back from your trip.

The easiest way to preserve flowers is to air-dry them. Remove leaves from the stems, tie them in a bunch at the base with a rubber band, and hang upside down from a hook or clothes hanger in a dark, dry, well-ventilated closet. To contain "shedding," cover the heads with a spacious brown paper bag. Flowers will dry in two to three weeks.

Single-rowed, flat-headed flowers such as pansies and violets are the best to press. Cut off the stem as close as possible to the base of the bud, then gently place the blooms on white, untextured blotting paper (available at stationery stores), making sure they don't overlap. Cover with a second sheet of blotting paper, sandwich between two pieces of stiff cardboard, and sandwich this sandwich with a small stack of heavy books. Store in a warm, dry room, and do not disturb for six weeks. No peeking! The longer the drying process, the better the color retention. Remove dried petals with a tweezers, and use to decorate thank-you notes and scrapbook pages.

Preserving Textiles

As soon as you take it off, hang up your gown and have one of your bridesmaids bring it to a cleaner who specializes in wedding dresses. The longer stains sit, the tougher they are to remove. When putting a dress away for a long-term storage, prevent folds and creases and make sure it can breathe. Wrap and line the dress with unbuffered acid-free tissue, stuff it with the insides of a hypoallergenic pillow, and place it in an acid-free, and unsealed, box. Avoid boxes with windows in the top because these let light in and can cause discoloration in one spot. Store the box in a dry, dark, cool place: Basements may be too

On the box top: Jennifer Lyn Garden and Christopher Staudenraus United in Marriage November 25, 2000

Our Wedding Day Keepsakes

to have and to hold

from this day

Chris

Jenny & Chris Staudenraus

damp, attics too hot. Humidity results in mildew, which eats away at fabric, and direct sunlight causes fibers to yellow. Inspect the dress annually, to make sure stains have not developed, and refold it along different lines to prevent creasing.

Gowns can also be stored in the upright position: Hanging allows them to oxidize evenly. Use a sealed-wood hanger padded with cotton batting, and cover the gown with a cotton muslin bag (you can make one out of about four yards of the fabric, first washed to shrink). Store it in a cool, dry closet.

Wedding shoes, the headpiece and veil, gloves, and the like should all be stored separately from the dress. Carefully wrap each item in unbuffered, acid-free tissue, and place them in an acid-free box. ✍

Keepsake Gifts

WEDDINGS ARE profoundly transformational events, turning mere man and woman into husband and wife, uniting them now and forever, from here to eternity, all the days of their lives and then some.

They're also a great way to get stuff.

After several bridal showers and a barrage of gifts at the reception (not to mention all those packages that keep arriving by mail), you and your groom have probably accumulated enough loot to stock the kitchen cabinets and bathroom closets of your humble abode. Now it's time to give back, and to give thanks, to all the amazing people who helped you pull off the whole wonderful, wild affair. Customarily, the couple gives gifts to the maid of honor, the best man, and the other members of the wedding party, including flower girls, ring bearers, and the officiant, if he or she is a close family friend. Parents deserve to be acknowledged for their support. And don't forget any hosts, such as the family friend who put up out-of-town guests in a spare bedroom or the uncle who held a celebratory barbecue.

While you're shopping for just the right presents, why not pick up a token of affection for your soon-to-be brand new husband? Send a small package ahead to the honeymoon hotel as a surprise. (Chances are your maid of honor will whisper a hint

PYRAMID BOX by Diane Hackley. Paper: scored triangle box, Magenta. Scissors: Fiskars. Elegant swirl and "Love" stamps: PrintWorks. Adhesive: Wonder Tape. Ribbon. Other: cat's eyes, Colorbox; paper flowers by Modern Romance. Fun idea to note: Diane rubbed the cat's eyes' pads on the paper box. She stamped the swirl on the lower edge of the box and the love stamp on the top of the box. After she put the box together, she tied the ribbon around the box and knotted it around the flowers.

PENTAGON BOX by Diane Hackley. Paper: scored box, Magenta. Scissors: Fiskars. Raindrops and swirls stamps: Hero Arts. Inkpads: Encore Metallics. Adhesive: Wonder Tape. Ribbon. Other: cat's eyes, Colorbox; paper flowers by Modern Romance. Fun idea to note: Diane chose a different color cats eye ink for the top and bottom of the box. She stamped the raindrops and swirls on the side of the box and the heart on the top and bottom. After she assembled the box, she tied the ribbon around the box and put the flowers in the middle.

EMBOSSED GIFT WRAP by Susana Espinosa/Rubber Stampede. Rubber stamps: Romantic Rose Small Bouquet and "To/From" by Rubber Stampede. Pencils: watercolors. Embossing: inkpad by Rubber Stampede; gold powder. Punch: small hole. Other: glue stick, ribbon. Fun idea to note: Susana cut the burgundy mulberry paper large enough to cover the gift box. She stamped three or four roses onto the paper, then embossed them, and continued stamping and embossing until the paper was completely stamped. She then wrapped the gift with this paper!

into his ear so that he'll do the same—one more reason she gets a special gift!)

Gifts are usually given out at the rehearsal dinner, but it may be more personal to offer each one individually at any other get-together during the week before the wedding.

That's the who. On to the what. Once upon a time, all the bridesmaids (and groomsmen) would receive the same item. Such uniformity helps to avoid any jealous outbreaks—after all, a wedding is an extremely emotional time, when sensitivities are heightened—and it's also more convenient to buy five identical silk scarves. But many couples now choose separate gifts for each attendant. It requires more thought and effort—and that's exactly the point. A

happy compromise of the two methods involves tailoring the same gift to different recipients. For example, the bride may buy an earrings-and-pendant set for her attendants, but select individual colors based on their birthstones.

Jewelry is a popular choice for women. A bracelet with a commemorative starter charm or a locket containing a flower from the bouquet are sentimental favorites, but bridesmaids will also appreciate flannel pajamas, theater tickets, or a certificate for a massage. Cufflinks or fountain pens are traditional presents for men. And parents might receive anything from a framed wedding portrait to a weekend getaway. The gift depends on the relationship: If a stellar best man has always wanted to learn how to snowboard, chip in for the equipment and the first few lessons.

Regardless of the cost of the gift, handcrafted accents add a personal element no amount of money can match. As an additional—or independent—present, wrap picture frames with textured papers, trim mats, and mount either a funny photo from the reception or a moving quotation. (*See pages 106–107 and Frames & Displays*). Mini-scrapbooks also make priceless gifts, particularly for those who couldn't attend the ceremony *(see Wedding Albums)*. Each can be edited with photos and journaling to tell a short story, whether it's the sequence of harried events leading up to the march down the aisle or the series of mishaps that took place during the reception.

Creative Wrapping

Inventive wrapping dresses up any present, and is especially effective on petit boxes, where the attention to detail is inversely proportionate to the tiny package (*Pyramid Box* and *Pentagon Box*, *page 98*). Create a shabby-chic contrast by embossing kraft wrapping paper with a monogram. To tie together a tiered stack of small cardboard boxes, weave ribbed grosgrain ribbon through tucked-in tops, bottoms, and sides—in one end, out the other. Or, if a box has a removable lid, punch two holes across the top, and two more on opposing sides of its bottom half. Thread ribbon to create a handle: The loop on top should be just big enough for a finger to hook. Secure the ribbon ends in nubby knots on the outer sides of the holes on the bottom half.

Ribbon or twine can also be used to attach paper emblems. Trim pleasing shapes—elegant ovals, voluptuous rounds, narrow rectangles—out of thick, colored cardstock, punch matching slots at both ends, and paint the recipient's initial in a whimsical script in the center of the cut-out. Thread the ribbon or twine through the slots so that it runs underneath the emblem, then tie around the box so that the letter is facing out from the top.

Antique buttons in opalescent materials make charming alternatives to bows. "Stitch" the button to its box top using a short piece of thin wire, then bend and twist the wire ends together beneath the lid. Once secure, loop ribbons from the base of the box up and around the button, and trim the fabric at a jaunty angle.

Fringed paper is undeniably festive. For small items such as cufflinks in an open container, loosely twist them in a few layered squares of colored tissue paper, then cut vertical strips into the top and "peel"

A GIFT FOR YOU by Kelly Edgerton. Gift tag: Hero Arts. Stickers: "Roses and Ribbon," Mrs. Grossman's Design Lines Photoessence. Computer font: CK Flair, "Wedding Alphabet" CD, *Creating Keepsakes*.

FOR MY FRIEND by Jenny Jackson. Stamp: D.O.T.S. Fun idea to note: Jenny crinkled the tissue paper and sprinkled it with gold embossing powder.

FOR MY MAID OF HONOR by Kelly Edgerton. Gift tag: Hero Arts. Stickers: "Hydrangea Stems," Mrs. Grossman's Photoessence. Computer font: CK Swirl, "Wedding Alphabet" CD, *Creating Keepsakes*.

A BRIDESMAID GIFT FOR YOU *(bottom left)* by Kelly Edgerton. Gift tag: Hero Arts. Stickers: Roses and Ribbon, Mrs. Grossman's Design Lines Photoessence. Computer font: CK Swirl, "Wedding Alphabet" CD, *Creating Keepsakes*.

A BRIDESMAID GIFT FOR YOU *(bottom right)* by Kelly Edgerton. Gift tag: Hero Arts. Stickers: Blossoms and Borders, PrintWorks. Computer font: CK Hearts, "Wedding Alphabets" CD, *Creating Keepsakes*.

them outward to create fronds (just like children do when they make rolled newspaper "trees"). Secure the center of the twist with thin wired ribbon or metallic twine, and nestle the tissued pouch in the base of the open box bottom.

When it comes to wrapping, it can actually be creative to think *inside* the box. A little extra attention to tissue liners makes a big difference. Tuck shocking squares of crimson, tangerine, and fuchsia into chaste white cartons, or print the liners with poetry verses, so that in addition to the expected card or name tag on the outside, guests will uncover a second note inside.

A combination of gradated colors saturates a present with the increasing intensity of a single shade. Begin with pale yellow paper, double with a tinted sunshine tissue, and tie with a ribbon as bright as a lemon. Or contrast solids with patterns. Band a

box wrapped in plain dark-colored paper with a light-colored belt featuring an ornate design. The pattern can echo the color of the plain paper or complement it. For example, a white ribbon with lime green graphics will energize a solid teal.

If giving attendants a gift certificate, seal it in a handmade envelope *(Thank-You Folder* and *Swirl Folder Card, page 108)*. Offer the same special presentation when giving them a letter stating that, in lieu of a present, a donation has been made in their name to a charitable organization. A photo matted with a simple paper frame and wrapped in vellum *(Pink Thank You, page 108)* makes a thoughtful add-on.

Care Packages

From far and farther, by plane, train, and automobile, they have come to celebrate your wedding. Thank the weary travelers who made the trek by outfitting their hotel room with a combination care package-survival kit designed to see them through the weekend. (Notify the concierge in advance, and ask a member of your wedding party to take the care packages to the hotel the morning that most guests arrive.)

Consider the particulars of the wedding when concocting a care package. City or country? Hot or cold? Several days or one night only? The answers to these questions will determine the carton's contents. Guests in a new city for a few days will appreciate a package containing a neighborhood map, a list of recommended restaurants and tourist sites, the name, address, and number of a 24-hour drugstore, a disposable camera, and, of course, the itinerary of wedding activities. But those who took the red-eye in and will be gone again by morning

ROSE THANK-YOU CARD by Heather Thatcher. Paper: white cardstock. Rose patterned paper: Paper Adventures. Plaid patterned paper: Paperbilities. Vellum with sparkles: Sonburn. Scissors: Microtip. Pens: Zig Writer, EK Success. Watercolor pencils: Design and Dewart. Fun idea to note: Heather makes her cards by folding plain white cardstock, then layering the front with patterned paper, textured paper, lettering, and other accents.

YELLOW AND RED FLOWERS THANK-YOU CARD by Heather Thatcher. Paper: white cardstock. Patterned paper: O scrap. Pens: Zig Writer, EK Success. Pencils: Berol Prismacolor.

GREEN LEAVES THANK-YOU CARD by Heather Thatcher. Paper: PrintWorks, white cardstock. Vine and leaf watercolor pattern paper: Colors By Design. Small green stripe paper: Susan Branch. Pens: Zig Millenium, EK Success. Pencils: Berol Prismacolor.

STRIPED THANK-YOU CARD by Heather Thatcher. Paper: white cardstock. Background paper: Provo Craft. Green stripe paper: Ever After. Pens: Zig Writer, EK Success. Pencils: Berol Prismacolor.

THANK-YOU CARD by Kelly Edgerton. Note cards: Hero Arts. Stickers: "Wedding Borders" and "Hearts and Flowers," Me & My BIG Ideas. Punch: 1/16" hole, Marvy Uchida. Pencils: Memory Pencils, EK Success. Computer font: CK Tulips, "Wedding Alphabet" CD, *Creating Keepsakes*. Other: raffia curling straw.

SOMETHING OLD by Patti Copenhaver. Rubber stamps: Romantic Rose, "Something Old," and small "Thank You" by Rubber Stampede. Embossing: inkpad by Rubber Stampede; gold powder. Pens/Pencils: gold pen; watercolor pencils. Adhesive: double stick tape; glue gun; photo corners. Gold ribbon. Fun idea to note: Patti used a gold pen to highlight the decorative paper edge.

PORTFOLIO CARD by Diane Hackley. Card: Hero Arts. Template: American Traditional Stencils. Florentine scroll stamp: Hero Arts. Small flower stamp: Magenta. Inkpads: Colorbox Metalextra, Encore Metallics. Adhesive: Zig 2-Way Glue. Fun idea to note: Diane stamped the gold ink background over the entire card.

GOLD & BLACK THANK-YOU CARD AND STATIONERY by Lanae Johnson. Adhesive: Photo Mounts, Creative Memories: glue pen, Sailor.

LOVE THANK YOU by Lanae Johnson. Fun idea to note: Lanae created the lettering on her computer. This thank-you note coordinated with her wedding invitation and program (see page 24)!

might prefer a crate of refreshing beverages, crunchy snacks—or comforting chocolate-chip cookies. Select items that don't require refrigeration, splurge for soda pop in retro bottles instead of common cans, but employ the art of "decanting" for the snacks: Buy cookies, candies, pretzels, or nuts inexpensively, in bulk, remove them from their commercial packaging, and rewrap individually. This allows lots of opportunities for creative expression—for example, back a clear plastic pouch with a card featuring a hand-lettered poem personally welcoming the guests, then pile in the peanuts and seal with a sticker.

For a chilly winter wedding, stuff woolly mittens or socks into a commemorative ceramic mug—do-it-yourself pottery studios have popped up all over the country—and pack with cocoa or tea bags. In summer, pack sunscreen, a cooling peppermint mist, and clusters of grapes and oranges. For guests traveling with children under 12, group stuffed animals, toy cars, little dolls, coloring books, and crayons to preoccupy children while their parents get settled.

To make a basic care package, begin with an inexpensive cardboard box, metal tin, or plywood carton. Stuff with tissue, straw, tinsel—anything that picks up the wedding's themes (if the groom is a banker, his pals will laugh at the sight of shredded accounting documents). In addition to the wedding itinerary, include a personal note and a "coupon booklet"—handcrafted strips of paper offering a ticket to the rehearsal dinner, a ride back to the airport from the best man, and so on.

Thank-You Notes

In this modern age, it's tempting to succumb to the convenience of the printer. But nothing can replace the handwritten thank-you note. A million etiquette mavens will say the same. So stock up on paper, shake out your wrist, and get writing.

Who gets a thank-you? Well, everyone. It is absolutely *de rigueur* to write a note for any gift received over the course of engagement parties, bridal showers, the reception, and into your first year as a married couple. It's also thoughtful to send complimentary notes to the vendors who got you through the day; florists, caterers, photographers, bakers, and beauticians rely on such letters of reference to promote their business.

To prepare for the task of writing a multitude of thank-you notes, create a form for yourself. (If organizing in advance of the ceremony, make it the master guest list.) Leave blank spaces for:

Name	RSVP Received
Address	Number in Party
Telephone	Gift
E-Mail	Thank-You Written
Invitation Sent	Thank-You Sent

A single page might be able to fit about four entries. Make multiple copies, hole-punch the pages, file them in a binder for easy reference, and every time you receive a gift, make a note. At showers, ask your maid of honor to snap Polaroids of each guest with the gift she brought. The photos will help to jog the memory a few months down the road. No, make that a few weeks down the road—staunch Miss Manners states that thank-you notes should be sent no later than one month after receipt but, considering how hectic life is, two months won't raise many eyebrows. The trick to staying on top of it is two-fold: First, at least until you hit critical mass, write and mail notes as you receive gifts; second, split the list with your husband. He responds to his people, you to yours, and, in special instances, one should add a postscript to the other's letter: "Arthur, after all the frat-house stories John has told me, it was great to finally meet the man behind the leg-

TORN-EDGE CARD by Lanae Johnson. Adhesive: Photo Mounts, Creative Memories; glue pen. Fun idea to note: Lanae scored and folded the burgundy cardstock, then used a metal ruler to tear the edge. She cut the tan parchment insert smaller than the card and adhered it with a thin line of glue. She created borders for the photo with burgundy and gold ribbed cardstock and mounted it to the card cover.

SQUARE THANK-YOU CARD by Lanae Johnson. Note cards: Noteworthy. Adhesive: Photo Mounts, Creative Memories. Fun idea to note: Lanae deliberately chose this "parting shot" of the bride and groom—a perfect choice for thank-you notes.

LASER CUT CARD by Lanae Johnson. Note cards: Strathmore. Laser cut: Scherenschnitte Design. Adhesive: Photo Mounts, Creative Memories. Fun idea to note: Lanae created a gold border slightly smaller than the window of the laser cut. She color copied a simple photo and adhered it to the laser cut, which she then mounted to the card cover.

OVAL PHOTO FRAME CARD by Lanae Johnson. Photo frame card: Kolo. Adhesive: Photo Mounts, Creative Memories. Fun idea to note: Lanae inserted, and secured, the photo into the cover. Nothing could be easier! You might consider creating individualized thank-you notes by tailoring the photo selection for each recipient.

PHOTO ENVELOPE by Lanae Johnson. Adhesive: Mounting Adhesive, Keep A Memory; Photo Mounts, Creative Memories. Fun idea to note: This photo sticker is a wonderful detail to add to your envelope flap. She used Mounting Adhesive to adhere her "sticker" to the envelope.

THANK-YOU FOLDER by Diane Hackley.
Scissors: Fiskars. Template: American
Traditional Stencils. Florentine scroll stamp:
Hero Arts. "Thank You" stamp: Denami
Design 1999. Inkpads: Encore Metallics.
Ribbon: Offray. Fun idea to note: Diane
stamped the background pattern on one side
of the paper before she folded it.

PINK THANK-YOU by Diane Hackley.
Vellum: Hero Arts. Scissors: Fiskars. Template:
Portfolio by American Traditional Stencils.
"Thank You" stamp: Denami Design 1999.
Inkpad: Encore Metallics. Ribbon: Offray.
Fun idea to note: Diane used the template's
directions to guide her when she dry
embossed the design onto the vellum.

SWIRL FOLDER CARD by Diane Hackley.
Fun idea to note: Diane attached a small
heart ornament to this elegant note card.

end!" Make thank-you notes an *après*-honeymoon activity, and tackle about ten a day. If you're feeling motivated, start them on the plane.

Promptness is particularly important if the gift arrived by mail or if the gift was monetary. Until they get a note, the givers will be wondering if their package was lost. When thanking someone for cash or a check, never use the words "cash" or "check," and definitely don't refer to the exact amount. Instead, specify how you and your husband plan to use the "generous gift."

Euphemisms also come in handy when the gift is hideous—that is, "unusual," "unique," "different," "a conversation piece." According to proper etiquette, a note must mention the item. But it's rude to even imply you're disappointed by a present. If you decide to return a gift, send a gracious note letting the giver know you've exchanged it. However, it's impolite to ask where an item was purchased, so if you don't know, let it go, write the note, and store the gift. It's also considered inappropriate to send a pre-printed card with nothing more than a signature (meaning no personal message). Notes can be short and sweet, but they should be special. Focus first on the person and your relationship, mention any reception hi-jinks or other shared memories, then refer to the gift—why you love it, where you'll put it, how it's just what you've always wanted.

Although it's perfectly sensible to use paper and envelopes bought in bulk with the invitation, hand-crafted cards send a personal message before the note inside is even read. Ribbons, raffia, embossing, stickers, lettering, and vellum overlays: All create one-of-a-kind keepsakes. Weddings are rich with cardmaking motifs—from a simple pink heart beaded on wire to a detailed stamp of a wedding dress *(below)*. Tiny ornaments are especially cute additions *(opposite)*. Seal deckled envelope flaps with a photo sticker *(Photo Envelope, page 107)*, or mat a portrait of that incredibly happy couple right on the cover of the card *(page 106)*.

BEADED CARD by Diane Hackley. Note cards: Hero Arts. Paper: Canson. Raindrops and swirls stamp: Hero Arts. Adhesive: Zig 2-Way Glue. Ribbon: Offray. Other: small pink beads; 26-gauge wire.

WEDDING DRESS CARD by Diane Hackley. Note cards: Denami Design. Vellum: Hero Arts. Wedding dress stamp: Uptown Rubber Stamps. Florentine scroll stamp: Hero Arts. Wired silver ribbon.

FLORAL THANK-YOU NOTE by Jenny Jackson. Rice paper: Freund-Mayer. Stamps: D.O.T.S.

EMBOSSED HEARTS by Jenny Jackson. Template: Lasting Impressions for Paper. Computer font: CK Script, "Best of Creative Lettering" CD Vol 1, *Creating Keepsakes*. Ribbon: Offray.

Wedding Photo Checklist

PHOTOGRAPHS ARE the ultimate wedding keepsake. The scrumptious cake is reduced to crumbs, the flowers fade and the seasons change, but photos preserve the precious moments of your unforgettable day. There are several different styles of wedding photographs: *Formal portraits* are the heirloom images of bride, groom, wedding party, and family members, posed individually and in groups. In *classic photographs*, the subjects are artfully but naturally posed. For example, the bride may view her reflection in the mirror, or gaze thoughtfully out the window. *Stock shots* record all the timeless traditions: the first dance, the cake-cutting, the bouquet toss. *Candids* catch the guests off guard, allowing everyone to be themselves and documenting the unique atmosphere of the gathering. By extension, *photojournalistic photos* chronicle the day as a news story, shooting events as they unfold rather than staging situations. And *artistic photography* incorporates specific techniques to give images a contemporary edge: Photos may be double-exposed, hand-tinted, silk-screened, or printed with the sprocket holes of the film visible. Most couples consider formal portraits and stock shots indispensable, then counterbalance these with more casual, candid photos of the reception. A combination of color and black-and-white images conveys both the temporality and timelessness of the occasion.

THE FOLLOWING LIST details many of the key images most couples want photographed for posterity. Modify the list to suit your plans, and present it to both your professional photographers and any friends or family members intent on clicking away at your ceremony and reception.

Portraits

- The bride
- The groom
- The bride and groom together
- The bride with her maid of honor
- The groom with his best man
- The bride with her parents, the groom with his
- The bride with her bridesmaids, the groom with his groomsmen
- The wedding party
- Bride and groom with their respective families
- Both families together for one group portrait
- "Generations": all the women or all the men in each family

Before the Ceremony

- Still-life of bridal gown, veil, gloves; the bride's vanity
- Bride dressing and arranging hair and makeup, with help of bridesmaids and mother
- Full-length photo of bride in gown viewing herself in the mirror

- Mother helping bride with one finishing touch—a stray tendril or dress strap

- Bride embracing mom before leaving for the ceremony

- Groom getting dressed, surrounded by groomsmen and father

- Groom knotting his tie, adjusting his boutonnière

- Groom in thoughtful moment with his father

- Bride and groom ready to go, each at their respective departure point

- Bride on the way to the ceremony: in the limo with dad, on horseback, hailing a taxi

The Ceremony

- The stillness of the ceremony space, before all the activity begins

- Still-life of ceremony details: the altar, the ketubah, a cluster of candles, flower arrangements marking the pews

- Guests streaming in

- The officiant talking with the groom and best man, soothing last-minute jitters

- Ushers escorting guests to their seats

- The groom at the altar—with his groomsmen, and a close-up of his nervous face

- Flower girl and ring bearer walking down the aisle

- Bridesmaids walking down the aisle

- Bride at the entrance (possibly in silhouette)

- Bride walking down the aisle with her escort

- Dad "giving away" his daughter

- Wide-angle shot of the wedding party at the altar

- Wide-angle and close-up shots of the guests during the ceremony—rapt with attention, laughing, crying, dozing, fanning themselves with their programs in the heat

- Readers reading, singers singing, musicians playing

- Zoom of bride and groom gazing into each other's eyes, exchanging vows

- Zoom of exchange of rings

- Zoom of the officiant

- Zoom of the kiss!

- Any ceremonial highlights: breaking the glass, jumping the broom

- Bride and groom rushing down the aisle

- Receiving line moments

- The rice (petal, seed, bubble) toss

- The getaway vehicle, strung with streamers, departing for the reception

The Reception

- The dramatic arrival of bride and groom

- Toasts

- Various friends and relatives in animated conversation

- Quiet moments between the parents of the bride and groom

- Rambunctious kids hiding under tablecloths, sneaking a taste of the cake

- The first dance between bride and groom

- The bride dancing with her dad, the groom with his mom

- The bride dancing with her bridesmaids

- The band

- The crowded, energetic dance floor

- Cutting the cake

- The bride feeds the groom, the groom feeds the bride

- The bouquet toss

- The garter toss

- The bride and groom dressed in their traveling clothes

- The great escape, with bride and groom waving good-bye

Helpful Hints for Amateur Photographers

- Shoot between the moments: A lot of humor is displayed as groups get ready for formal portraits and disassemble afterward.

- Shoot sequences: First the couple crosses the threshold of the ceremony site, then they look up at the cloud of rice headed their way, then they duck and laugh under the shower.

- Vary close-ups with wide-angle shots: Close-ups capture expressions and emotions; wide shots capture the overall energy of the event.

- Shoot with selective focus: Use shallow depth of field, focus on a face, and blur the background.

- Incorporate surprising elements into stock shots: Maybe there's one lone fellow vying for the bride's bouquet, or a couple of kids imitating the first dance of the bride and groom.

- Maintain a sense of romance, a sense of humor, and a sense of narrative: These photos will tell the story of the day.

- Vary perspective: close-crops, full-lengths, groups shots, individuals, from above, below, and behind.

- Don't forget the details: Capture all the elements the couple has worked so hard on—the table settings, the centerpieces, the favors, the cake.

- Remember that, to fit everybody into group shots, the camera must be elevated *or* the group must stand in tiers, up the steps of the church, for example.

- Check for "false attachment"—the appearance of a tree branch or telephone pole growing out of someone's head

- When shooting into mirrors, refrain from using the flash in order to avoid a "hot spot" on the print, and either duck down or shoot from the side, so that your reflection doesn't show up in the photo, too!

- When shooting candlelight: Get as close as possible to your subject, and use the fastest speed film your camera can take (e.g., ISO 800–1000).

- To shoot silhouettes, position the sun behind your subjects and don't use the flash.

Finally, as New York City-based wedding photographer Alfonse Pagano jokes, "Don't forget to put film in the camera!"

Origami Star Box

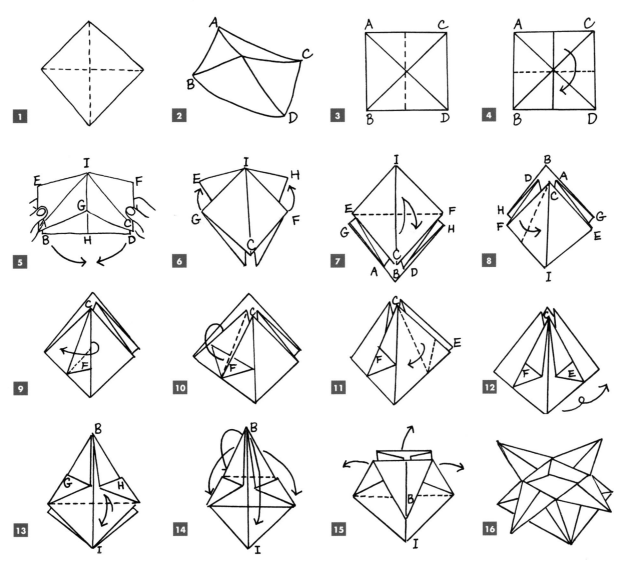

1. Crease square paper diagonally to form an X and unfold. **2.** View of outer side. Paper should have outer side up for next steps. **3.** Fold in half down the middle and unfold. **4.** Fold in half the other way and leave in this position. **5.** Hold horizontally and push sides together so that vertical folds at center buckle outward at G and H. Grab G with left thumb and make a pleat between G and E. Grab H with right fingers and make a pleat between F and H. **6.** Flatten front panel into a diamond shape. **7.** Fold single layer corner C up and unfold. **8.** Turn upside-down. Fold edge FC towards center crease. Unfold. **9.** Open corner F and squash it down so that . . . **10.** . . . the inside layers are exposed and an upside-down triangle forms **11.** Pinch upside-down triangle so that flaps of FC fold down. **12.** Repeat steps 8-11 with remaining three corners. **13.** Turn up bottom corner to fold between widest two points and unfold. **14.** Fold down single point B. **15.** Repeat, folding down each point of the star in a similar way. **16.** Open up box, flattening bottom.

Wedding Quotes

Scripture

LET LOVE BE genuine; hate what is evil, hold fast to what is good; love one another with brotherly affection; outdo one another in showing honor. Never flag in zeal, be aglow with the Spirit, serve the Lord. Rejoice in your hope, be patient in tribulation, be constant in prayer. Contribute to the needs of the saints, practice hospitality.

— ROMANS 12:9–13

PUT ON THEN, as God's chosen ones, holy and beloved, compassion, kindness, lowliness, meekness, and patience, forbearing one another and, if one has a complaint against another, forgiving each other; as the Lord has forgiven you, so you also must forgive. And above all these put love, which binds everything together in perfect harmony.

— COLOSSIANS 3:12–13

"These things I have spoken to you, that my joy may be in you, and that your joy may be full.

"This is my commandment, that you love one another as I have loved you. Greater love has no man than to lay down his life for his friends. You are my friends if you do what I command you. No longer do I call you servants, for the servant does not know what his master is doing; but I have called you friends, for all that I have heard from my Father I have made known to you. You did not choose me, but I chose you and appointed you that you should go and bear fruit and that your fruit should abide; so that whatever you ask the Father in my name, he may give it to you. This I command you, to love one another."

— JOHN 15:11–17

*Then God said, "Let us make man in our
image, after our likeness; and let them
have dominion over the fish of the sea, and over the
birds of the air, and over the cattle, and over
all the earth, and over every creeping thing that
crawls upon the earth." So God created man in his
own image, in the image of God he created him;
male and female he created them. And God blessed
them, and God said to them, "Be fruitful and
multiply, and fill the earth and subdue it; and have
dominion over the fish of the sea and over
the birds of the air and over every living thing that
moves upon the earth." And God said, "Behold,
I have given you every plant yielding seed which is
upon the face of all the earth, and every tree
with seed in its fruit; you shall have them for food.
And to every beast of the earth, and to every
bird of the air, and to everything that crawls on the
earth, everything that has the breath of life,
I have given every green plant for food." And it
was so. And God saw everything that he had made,
and behold, it was good. And there was evening
and there was morning, a sixth day.*

— GENESIS 1:26–31

I have come into my garden,
My sister, my bride,
I have gathered the myrrh and spices,
I have eaten from the honeycomb,
I have drunk the milk and the wine.

Feast, friends, and drink
Till you are drunk with love!

—FROM THE SONG OF SONGS

*Blessed are the man and the woman
    who have grown beyond themselves
    and have seen through their separations.
They delight in the way things are
    and keep their hearts open, day and night.
They are like trees planted near flowing rivers,
    which bear fruit when they are ready.
Their leaves will not fall or wither.
    Everything they do will succeed.*

—PSALM I

Sing to the Lord, all creatures!
    Worship him with your joy;
        praise him with the sound of your laughter.
Know that we all belong to him,
    that he is our source and our home.
Enter his light with thanksgiving;
    fill your hearts with this praise.
For his goodness is beyond comprehension,
    and his deep love endures forever.

—PSALM 100
(used at traditional Jewish ceremony)

Poetry

. . . the earth says hello to us
The day has all our rainbows
The fireplace is lit with our eyes
And the ocean celebrates our marriage

— PAUL ELUARD
from "Between Us a New Morning"

I have been here before,
But when or how I cannot tell:
I know the grass beyond the door,
The sweet, keen smell,
The sighing sound, the lights around the shore.

You have been mine before,
How long ago I may not know:
But just when at that swallow's soar
Your neck turned so,
Some veil did fall, I knew it all of yore.

Has this been thus before?
And shall not thus time's eddying flight
Still with our lives our love restore
In death's despite,
And day and night yield on delight once more?

— DANTE GABRIEL ROSSETTI
"Sudden Light"

. . . love me for love's sake, that evermore
Thou mayest love on, through love's eternity . . .

When our two souls stand up erect and strong,
Face to face, silent, drawing nigh and nigher,
Until the lengthening wings break into fire
At either curvèd point—what bitter wrong
Can the earth do to us, that we should not long
Be here contented? Think. In mounting higher,
The angels would press on us and aspire
To drop some golden orb of perfect song
Into our deep, dear silence. Let us stay
Rather on earth, beloved—where the unfit
Contrarious moods of men recoil away
And isolate pure spirits and permit
A place to stand and love in for a day,
With darkness and the death-hour rounding it.

How do I love thee? Let me count the ways.
I love thee to the depth and breadth and height
My soul can reach, when feeling out of sight
For the ends of Being and ideal Grace.
I love thee to the level of everyday's
Most quiet need, by sun and candle-light.
I love thee freely, as men strive for Right;
I love thee purely, as they turn from Praise.
I love thee with the passion put to use
In my old griefs, and with my childhood's faith.
I love thee with a love I seemed to lose
With my lost saints,—I love thee with the breath,
Smiles, tears, of all my life!—and, if God choose,
I shall but love thee better after death.

— ELIZABETH BARRETT BROWNING
from *Sonnets from the Portuguese*

. . . I come to you
lost, wholly trusting, as a man who goes
into the forest unarmed. . . . I rest in peace
in you, when I arrive at last.

— WENDELL BERRY
from "The Country of Marriage"

your slightest look easily
will unclose me

though i have closed myself
as fingers,

you open always petal by petal
myself as Spring opens

(touching skilfully, mysteriously)
her first rose

— E. E. CUMMINGS
from "Somewhere I Have Never Travelled"

Two happy lovers make one single bread,
one single drop of moonlight in the grass.
When they walk, they leave two shadows that merge,
and they leave one single sun blazing in their bed.

— PABLO NERUDA
from Sonnet XLVIII

For one human being to

love another human being: that is

perhaps the most difficult

task that has been entrusted to us,

the ultimate task, the final

test and proof, the work for which all

other work is merely preparation.

— RAINER MARIA RILKE
from *Letters to a Young Poet*

During winter we will ride in a little red carriage
With cushions of blue.
We will be so happy. And a nest of stolen kisses
Will soften the turn at each corner.

You shut your eyes and no longer look
        out the window
At the grimacing shadows of the night,
Hordes of gloomy nightmares, populated with
Black demons and black wolves.

And then you suddenly feel with a panic—
A little kiss, like a scared spider crawl
Across your cheek to your neck—

You say to me: "Look!" as you turn your head
—And I take forever as I try to find the beast.
—What a marvelous ride!

— ARTHUR RIMBAUD
"A Winter Dream"

Turn me like a waterwheel turning a millstone.
Plenty of water, Living Water.
Keep me in one place and scatter the love.
Leaf moves in a wind, straw drawn
    toward amber,
all parts of the world are in love,
but they do not tell their secrets:
    Cows grazing
on a sacramental table, ants whispering in
    Solomon's ear.
Mountains mumbling an echo. Sky, calm.
If the sun were not in love, he would have
    no brightness,
the side of the hill no grass on it.
The ocean would come to rest
    somewhere.
Be a lover as they are, that you come
    to know
your Beloved. Be faithful that you may know
Faith. The other parts of the universe did
    not accept
the next responsibility of love as you can.
They were afraid they might make a mistake
with it, the inspired knowing
that springs from being in love.

—JELALUDDIN RUMI
{Rumi Example 1.}

The minute I heard my first love story
I started looking for you, not knowing
how blind that was.

Lovers don't finally meet somewhere.
They're in each other all along.

—JELALUDDIN RUMI
{Rumi Example 2.}

THIS MARRIAGE
be wine with halvah, honey dissolving in milk.

THIS MARRIAGE
be the leaves and fruit of a date tree.

THIS MARRIAGE
be women laughing together for days on end.

THIS MARRIAGE
a sign for us to study.

THIS MARRIAGE,
beauty.

THIS MARRIAGE,
a moon in a light-blue sky.

THIS MARRIAGE,
this silence fully mixed with spirit.

—JELALUDDIN RUMI
{Rumi Example 3.}

Let me not to the marriage of true minds
Admit impediments: love is not love,
Which alters when it alteration finds,
Or bends with the remover to remove;
O, no! it is an ever-fixèd mark,
That looks on tempests and is never shaken;
It is the star to every wandering bark,
Whose worth's unknown, although his height be
    taken.
Love's not Time's fool, though rosy lips and cheeks
Within his bending sickle's compass come;
Love alters not with his brief hours and weeks,
But bears it out even to the edge of doom.
    If this be error and upon me proved,
    I never writ, nor no man ever loved.

—WILLIAM SHAKESPEARE
Sonnet 116

It is true love because . . .
I do not resent watching the Green Bay Packers
Even though I am philosophically opposed to
   football . . .

—JUDITH VIORST
from "True Love"

So different, this man
And this woman:
A stream flowing
In a field.

—WILLIAM CARLOS WILLIAMS
"Marriage"

So are you to my thoughts as food to life,
Or as sweet-season'd showers are to the ground;
And for the peace of you I hold such strife
As 'twixt a miser and his wealth is found;
Now proud as an enjoyer, and anon
Doubting the filching age will steal his treasure;
Now counting best to be with you alone,
Then better'd that the world may see my pleasure:
Sometime all full with feasting on your sight,
And by and by clean starved for a look;
Possessing or pursuing no delight,
Save what is and or must from you be took.
   Thus do I pine and surfeit day by day,
   Or gluttoning on all, or all away.

—WILLIAM SHAKESPEARE
Sonnet 75

Proverbs

Love is the only flower that grows and blossoms
without the aid of the seasons

—KAHLIL GIBRAN

I will be great, and you rich, because
we love each other
—VICTOR HUGO

Love never dies of want, but often of indigestion

—NINON DE LENCLOS

Life is a long sleep and love is its dream.
—MUSSET

The only true language in the world is a kiss.

—MUSSET

The heart has its reasons that
the mind knows not.
—PASCAL

Love is not the act of looking at each other but of
looking together in the same direction.

—SAINT-EXUPÉRY

Love teaches even donkeys to dance.

— FRENCH PROVERB

The Tao begins in the relation between
man and woman, and ends
in the infinite vastness of the universe.

— TZU-SSU

The torch of love is lit in the kitchen.

— FRENCH PROVERB

Other Texts

Now you will feel no rain,
for each of you will be a shelter to the other.

Now you will feel no cold,
for each of you will be warmth to the other.

Now there is no loneliness for you;
now there is no more loneliness.

Now you are two bodies,
but there is only one life before you.

Go now to your dwelling place,
to enter into your days together.

And may your days be good
and long on the earth.

— APACHE SONG

Rising Sun! when you shall shine,

Make this house happy,

Beautify it with your beams;

Make this house happy,

God of Dawn! your white blessings spread;

Make this house happy.

Guard the doorway from all evil;

Make this house happy.

White corn! Abide herein;

Make this house happy.

Soft wealth! May this hut cover much;

Make this house happy.

Heavy Rain! Your virtues send;

Make this house happy.

Corn Pollen! Bestow content;

Make this house happy.

May peace around this family dwell;

Make this house happy.

— NAVAJO CHANT

For the mind in harmony with the Tao,
     all selfishness disappears.
With not even a trace of self-doubt,
     you can trust the universe completely.
All at once you are free,
     with nothing left to hold on to.
All is empty, brilliant,
     perfect in its own being.
In the world of things as they are,
     there is no self, no non-self.
If you want to describe its essence,
     the best you can say is "Not-two."
In this "Not-two" nothing is separate,
     and nothing in the world is excluded.
The enlightened of all times and places
     have entered into this truth.
In it there is no gain or loss;
     one instant is ten thousand years.
There is no here, no there;
     infinity is right before your eyes.
The tiny is as large as the vast
     when objective boundaries have vanished;
The vast is as small as the tiny
     when you don't have external limits.
Being is an aspect of non-being;
     non-being is no different from being.
Until you understand this truth,
     you won't see anything clearly.
One is all; all are one.
     when you realize this, what reason for
holiness or wisdom?
The mind of absolute trust
     is beyond all thoughts, all striving,
is perfectly at peace, for in it
     there is no yesterday, no today, no tomorrow.

     — "THE MIND OF ABSOLUTE TRUST";
     Seng-ts'an, Third Founding Teacher of Zen

"All night the cicada chirps;
all day the grasshopper jumps.
Before I saw my love,
my heart was confused.
But now that I have seen him,
now that I have met him,
my heart is calm."

"I climbed the southern hill
to pick the fern shoots.
Before I saw my love,
my heart was troubled.
But now that I have seen her,
now that I have met her,
my heart is at peace.

"I climbed the southern hill
to pick the bracken shoots.
Before I saw my love,
my heart was sad.
But now that I have seen her,
now that I have met her,
my heart is serene."

—FROM THE CHINESE
BOOK OF SONGS

Resources

General Suppliers

Many suppliers on this list are wholesalers but will direct you to stores in your area that carry their products.

Alto's EZ Mat, Inc.
Matting tools and supplies; excellent matting instructions on website.
703 N. Wenas
Ellensburg, WA 98926
800/225-2497
509/962-3127 (fax)
www.altosezmat.com

The Broom Lady
Handcrafted wedding brooms, supplies for and information about African American wedding traditions.
6 West Cary Street
Richmond, VA 23220
(877) 586-7164 (phone/fax)

Books by Hand
Kits for making accordion books, albums, and picture frames.
P.O. Box 80354
Albuquerque, NM 87198
(505) 255-3534
www.paperqueen.com

Cardeaux
Imprintable invitations and place cards.
629 17th Avenue West
Bradenton, FL 34205
(800) 226-8905
(941) 748-4727
(941) 748-7915

D.J. Inkers
Computer fonts, as well as stamps and stickers.
P.O. Box 467
Coalville, UT 84017
(800) 944-4680
www.djinkers.com

EK Success Ltd.
Stamps, stickers, permanent-ink pens and markers, red-eye pens and various scrapbooking supplies.
P.O. Box 1141
Clifton, NJ 07014-1141
(800) 524-1349

Embossing Arts Co.
Stamps, punches, papers, embossing powders, glues, stencils, and various accessories.
P.O. Box 439
31961 Rolland Drive
Tangent, Oregon 97389
(541) 928-9898
(541) 928-9977 (fax)

Forever Yours/ Keepsafe Systems
Information about and materials for the storage and preservation of gowns and other sensitive items.
570 King Street West
Toronto, Ontario
M5V 1M3
(800) 683-4696
(416) 703-4696
(416) 703-5991 (fax)
www.gowncare.com

Fiskars
Decorative scissors, red-eye pens, and various scrapbooking supplies.
305 84th Avenue
South Wausau, WI 54401
(715) 842-2091`
(715) 848-3657 (fax)
www.fiskars.com

Frances Meyer Inc.
Stickers.
PO Box 3088
Savannah, GA 31402-3088
(800) FRANCES
(912) 748-8419 (fax)

Freund-Mayer

Brass and glass seals, sealing wax, rice paper napkins, gift wrap, place cards, deluxe napkins, doilies, and various other accessories.

P.O. Box 515
190 Belle Mead Road
Suites 3 & 4
East Setauket, NY 11733
(800) 783-0615
(631) 941-1378

Hanko Designs

Decorative paper for origami.

875A Island Drive #186
Alameda, CA 94502
(510) 523-5603 (tel/fax)
hanko@hankodesigns.com

Hero Arts

Rubber stamps, blank cards, tinted vellum.

1343 Powell Street
Emeryville, CA 94608
(800) 822-4376
(800) 441-3632 (fax)
www.heroarts.com

Highsmith Inc.

Acid-free, corrugated cardboard box products.

W5527 Highway 106
PO Box 800
Fort Atkinson, WI 53538-0800
(800) 554-4661
(800) 558-9332 (fax)

Hiller Books and Binders

Acid-free scrapbook binders and paper.

631 North 400 West
Salt Lake City, Utah 84103
(801) 521-2411
(801) 521-2420 (fax)

Hot Off the Press Inc.

Patterned paper.

1250 NW Third
Canby, OR 97013
(503) 266-9102
(503) 266-8749 (fax)

K & Company

Wedding albums, frames, decorative mats, binders, scrapbook papers, stickers.

7441 West 161st Street
Stilwell, KS 66085
(913) 685-1458
(913) 851-2061 (fax)

Kolo

Large photo albums, mini-albums, and journals.

241 Asylum Street
Hartford, CT 06103
(860) 547-0367
(860) 547-0589 (fax)
www.kolo-usa.com

Lasting Impressions for Paper, Inc.

Supplies for dry embossing.

585 West 2600 South, Suite A
Bountiful, Utah 84010
(800) 9EMBOSS (to place an order)
(801) 298-1983 (fax)

Limited Edition Rubber Stamps

Rubber stamps.

1514 Stafford Street
Redwood City, CA 94063
(650) 299-9700
(650) 261-9300 (fax)
info@limitededitions.com
www.LimitedEditionRS.com

Magenta

Rubber stamps, journals and notebooks, gift boxes for stamping.

351, rue Blain
Mont Saint-Hilaire, QC
J3H 3B4 Canada
(514) 446-5253
(514) 464-6353 (fax)
(800) 565-5254 (orders only)

Me & My BIG Ideas

Stickers.

23091 Antonio Parkway
Rancho Santa Margarita, CA 92688
(949) 589-4007
(949) 589-6418 (fax)

My Sentiments Exactly
Rubber stamps, embossing powder.
4695 Centauri Road, Suite 100
Colorado Springs, CO 80919
(800) 307-8305
(719) 522-0797 (fax)
info@sentiments.com

Natural Paper Company
Wedding invitation kits.
16600 Harbor Boulevard
Fountain Valley, CA 92708
(714) 775-1449 (fax)

Papers by Catherine
Wedding invitation kits.
11328 South Post Oak #108
Houston, Texas 77035
(713) 723-3334
(713) 723-4749 (fax)

Paper Complements
Silk-finished cardstock, templates.
The Crafter's Workshop
116 S. Central Avenue
Elmsford, NY 10523
(914) 345-2838
(914) 345-0575 (fax)

Personal Stamp Exchange
Rubber stamps, paper, templates.
360 Sutton Place
Santa Rosa, CA 95407
(707) 588-8058
(707) 588-7476 (fax)
www.psxstamps.com

Provo Craft Design Center
Patterned paper, stickers, and various accessories.
295 West Center Street
Provo, UT 84601
(801) 373-6838

Riley Mountain Products, Inc.
Victorian photo mats, Mastermount products, accessories.
10 Water Street
Antrim, NH 03440
(800) 243-8145 ext. 150
(603) 588-3334 (fax)

Rubber Romance
Rubber stamps.
4554 Patricia Circle
Cypress, CA 90630
(888) 424-1222
Rubberromance@huntington beach.com

Rubber Stampede, Inc.
Rubber stamps for paper and home decor.
967 Stanford Avenue
Oakland, CA 94608
(510) 420-6845
(510) 420-6888 (fax)

Scherenschnitte Design
Laser-cut frames and paper.
1910 A Highway 7
Oroville, WA 98844
(509) 476-5480
sdlcorp@yahoo.com

Solum World Paper
Handmade, hand-printed papers, gift boxes, and stationery.
868 San Antonio
Palo Alto, CA 94303
(650) 812-7584
(650) 812-7583 (fax)

SpotPen
Red-eye removal pens.
30821 16 Place SW, Suite C
Federal Way, WA 98023
(253) 874-9025
(240) 208-4775 (fax)

Stampa Rosa, Inc.
Rubber stamps.
60 Maxwell Court
Santa Rosa, CA 95401
(800) 554-5755
(707) 570-0868 (fax)
www.stamparosa.com

Stampendous, Inc.
Rubber stamps, paper, inks.
1240 North Red Gum
Anaheim, CA 92806-1820
(800) 869-0474
(714) 688-0297 (fax)
www.stampendous.com

Wallies
Wallpaper cutouts.
P.O. Box 210
Belmont, VT 05730
(800) 255-2762 ext. 373
(802) 492-3450 (fax)
www.wallies.com

Archival Supplies

Archival Image
(800) 688-2485
Plastic sleeves, presentation materials, and professional photography supplies.

Gaylord Bros.
(800) 634-6307
Storage binders, boxes, acid-free tissue.

International Fabricare Institute
(301) 622-1900
Fabric and clothing preservation information.
12251 Tech Road
Silver Spring, MD 20904

Metal Edge
(800) 862-2228
Acid-free boxes, storage supplies, binders, papers, and the Image Archival Freezer Kit for storing negatives.

Preservation Source
(801) 278-7880
Supplies for preserving paper documents, photographs, and textiles.

University Products, Inc.
(800) 628-1912
Boxes, papers, acid-free tissue, books, red-eye pens.

Books and Software

The Art of Creative Lettering: 50 Amazing New Alphabets You Can Make for Scrapbooks, Cards, Invitations, and Signs
by Becky Higgins.
Alphabets, patterns, techniques, and ideas for using lettering in scrapbook pages and on cards.
Orem, UT: Creating Keepsakes Books, 1999
www.creatingkeepsakes.com (888) 247-5282.

The Best of Creative Lettering CD, Volumes 1 and 2
Automatically-installing CDs with the alphabets, phrases, and clip art from Creating Keepsakes's *Creative Lettering column.*
Orem, UT: Creating Keepsakes, Inc., 1999
(888) 247-5282

Wedding Alphabets CD
Automatically-installing CD with 15 fonts from The Art of Creative Lettering *by Becky Higgins that are suited to wedding projects.*
Orem, UT: Creating Keepsakes, Inc., 2000
(888) 247-5282

Wedding Scrapbooks: 80 New Ways to Tie the Knot
Special issue of Creating Keepsakes *scrapbook magazine devoted to wedding scrapbook page ideas.*
Orem, UT: Creating Keepsakes, 1998
(888) 247-5282

Index

Other Titles from
Creating Keepsakes Books

www.creatingkeepsakes.com

THE ART OF CREATIVE LETTERING: 50 AMAZING NEW ALPHABETS YOU CAN MAKE FOR SCRAPBOOKS, CARDS, INVITATIONS, AND SIGNS by Becky Higgins with Siobhán McGowan. Easy instructions for making creative alphabets, with lots of samples for inspiration. Paperback $19.95, ISBN 1-929180-11-x. Hardcover $25.00, ISBN 1-929180-10-1.

BABY ALPHABETS CD by Becky Higgins. An easy-to-use CD for projects involving babies and young children. $14.95, ISBN 1-929180-26-8.

MOM'S LITTLE BOOK OF DISPLAYING CHILDREN'S ART by Lisa Bearnson with Julie Taboh. Seventy-five ideas for creatively displaying your children's creations. Hardcover $16.95, ISBN 1-929180-16-0.

MOM'S LITTLE BOOK OF PHOTO TIPS by Lisa Bearnson and Siobhán McGowan. A mom-to-mom advice book that's 100% nontechnical and emphasizes the creative side of photography. Hardcover $16.95, ISBN 1-929180-12-8.

WEDDING ALPHABET CD by Becky Higgins. Fifteen fonts for wedding projects in an easy-to-use CD format. $14.95, ISBN 1-929180-25-x.